CONTENTS

1

WOODY ALLEN: THE POETRY OF THE JOKE

BY GLENN HOPP

WOODY ALLEN: DIE POESIE DES WITZES

WOODY ALLEN: L'ART DE LA FACÉTIE

WOODY ALLEN: THE POETRY OF THE JOKE

by Glenn Hopp

The Italian word *sprezzatura* is hard to define. It was coined by Baldesar Castiglione in *The Book of the Courtier* (1528) as a way of identifying the magical quality that stamped those belonging to the Renaissance's inner ring, the 16th-century version of the beautiful people. It describes the artful nonchalance of someone who can do difficult things easily, who can make something studied and worked out seem tossed off. In the celebrity culture of today, we might say that *sprezzatura* is a key component of charisma.

A realization of Woody Allen's *sprezzatura* always comes as a surprise. We have to get used to the idea that behind the familiar comic persona of the bumbling neurotic is a serious cinematic artist who meticulously controls nearly every aspect of his films. This comic persona of Allen's little schlemiel has ties to Charlie Chaplin's Little Tramp in his forlorn, outsider status. His verbal style and comic braggadocio derive from the screen humor of Bob Hope, whose work Allen idolizes. But the crafted screen character is just one of many seemingly effortless things made by Woody Allen, the creative artist.

The first was probably the joke. Allen supplied quips to New York newspaper columnists from age 16. Soon he was writing jokes for comedians and for many shows in the early days of television (Neil Simon's brother Danny was an invaluable mentor/cowriter). Eventually, Allen began working on stand-up routines for himself, and with that success came publishing casuals in *The New Yorker*, writing two successful Broadway comedies, and directing his early, joke-centered films. But even then the artist behind the joke machine respected the labor needed to make it look easy, as Allen told biographer Eric Lax: "In a very compressed way, you express a thought or a feeling and it's dependent on balancing the words ... For example, 'It's not that I'm afraid of dying, I just don't want to be there when it happens.' ... If you use one word more or less it's not as good ... This is what

PORTRAIT (1966)

"The only thing standing between me and greatness is me."
Woody Allen in 2005

poets do. They're not working their meters by the numbers, they're feeling." It's an apt analogy. The original meaning of the word *poem* is "a made thing." Both poem and joke, if crafted well, also share another definition: saying much with little.

Allen progressed from joke comedy to psychological comedy. *Annie Hall*, *Manhattan*, and *Hannah and Her Sisters* mine the deeper humor based on personality and show an artistic advance from the skitlike nature of *Everything You Always Wanted to Know About Sex*, *Sleeper*, and *Love and Death*. A good example of this higher comedy appears in a split-screen scene from *Annie Hall*. Annie and Alvy are both in therapy sessions and have both just been asked how often they have sex with each other. Alvy: "Hardly ever! I'd say two or three times a week." Annie: "Constantly! I'd say two or three times a week." This higher comedy (what George Meredith called "thoughtful laughter") enriches emotion and fosters seriousness. Allen's work has also come to reveal the poignant emotional mix of tragicomedy in the charm and fantasy of *The Purple Rose of Cairo*, the nostalgia of *Radio Days*, the multiple plots of *Crimes and Misdemeanors*, and the bittersweet tone of *Alice*.

The latest surprise of Allen's creative *sprezzatura* has been the tragic vision of *Match Point*, his most accomplished serious film. Allen's artistic idols also include Eugene O'Neill and Ingmar Bergman, but his reverence for them may have initially stifled his originality. His dramatic work (*Interiors*, *September*, and *Another Woman*) has required a longer evolution before revealing the *sprezzatura* of seeming to be natural. Allen himself, for example, admitted to Eric Lax in a book of interviews that the dialogue in *Interiors* derives more from the stiffly formal subtitles on Bergman movies than from idiomatic English. The critical and commercial success of *Match Point* has finally earned for Allen the appreciation and respect he previously lacked as a writer-director of dramatic films.

ENDPAPERS/VOR- UND NACHSATZBLÄTTER/PAGES
DE GARDE
**ON THE SET OF 'EVERYTHING YOU ALWAYS
WANTED TO ASK ABOUT SEX* (*BUT WERE
AFRAID TO ASK)' (1972)**

PAGES 6/7
**STILL FROM 'A MIDSUMMER NIGHT'S SEX
COMEDY' (1982)**

PAGES 2/3
STILL FROM 'MANHATTAN' (1979)

PAGE 8
PORTRAIT (1967)

PAGE 4
PORTRAIT FOR 'MANHATTAN' (1979)

OPPOSITE/RECHTS/CI-CONTRE
STILL FROM 'BANANAS' (1971)

WOODY ALLEN: DIE POESIE DES WITZES

von Glenn Hopp

Der italienische Begriff *sprezzatura* ist schwer zu definieren. Geprägt hat ihn Baldassare Castiglione in seinem *Libro del cortegiano* (*Der Hofmann*, 1528), um jene Aura des Magischen zu beschreiben, die höfische Renaissancemenschen umgab – das Pendant des 16. Jahrhunderts zu den „beautiful people" von heute. Er beschreibt die kunstvolle Nonchalance eines Menschen, dem schwierige Dinge leichtfallen und der es schafft, harte Fleißarbeit mühelos dahingeworfen erscheinen zu lassen. In der Promikultur von heute könnte man sagen, dass *sprezzatura* ein wichtiger Bestandteil des Charismas ist.

Die Umsetzung von Woody Allens *sprezzatura* ist immer überraschend. Wir müssen uns erst an den Gedanken gewöhnen, dass hinter der bekannten komischen Figur des linkischen Neurotikers ein ernsthafter Filmkünstler steckt, der jeden Aspekt seiner Filme akribisch steuert. Allens komische Figur des kleinen Schlemihls ist als einsamer Außenseiter mit Charlie Chaplins kleinem Tramp verwandt, während sein verbaler Ausdruck und seine spaßige Prahlerei vom Leinwandhumor Bob Hopes herrühren, dessen Werk Allen vergöttert. Aber die sorgsam ausgearbeitete Filmfigur ist nur eines der vielen eben nur scheinbar leichten Dinge, die der Kunstschöpfer Woody Allen hervorgebracht hat.

Am Anfang stand vermutlich der Witz. Im Alter von 16 Jahren lieferte Allen einigen New Yorker Zeitungskolumnisten Gagvorlagen. Bald danach schrieb er Witze für Komiker und viele der frühen Fernsehshows (Neil Simons Bruder Danny gehörte zu seinen wertvollsten Kollegen und Förderern). Schließlich begann Allen, sich eigene Stand-up-Nummern auszudenken, und im Kielwasser dieses Erfolgs folgten Beiträge für den *New Yorker*, zwei erfolgreiche Broadway-Komödien und seine frühen Filme, bei denen noch die Gags im

PORTRAIT FOR 'LOVE AND DEATH' (1975)
Like Bob Hope in 'The Road to Rio' (1947), Woody appears as a human cannonball. / Wie Bob Hope in *Der Weg nach Rio* (1947) spielt Allen eine menschliche Kanonenkugel. / Comme son héros Bob Hope dans *En route pour Rio* (1947), Woody se transforme en boulet de canon humain.

„Das Einzige, was zwischen mir und wahrer Größe steht, bin ich."
Woody Allen 2005

Mittelpunkt standen. Doch schon damals hatte der Künstler hinter der Gagmaschine großen Respekt vor der Mühe, die es kostete, einen Gag locker erscheinen zu lassen, wie er seinem Biografen Eric Lax erzählte: „Man drückt einen Gedanken oder ein Gefühl in einer sehr komprimierten Form aus, und es hängt ab von der Balance der Worte … Zum Beispiel: ‚Nicht, dass ich Angst vorm Sterben hätte – ich möchte nur nicht da sein, wenn's passiert.‘ … Wenn man ein Wort mehr oder weniger hineinbringt, ist der Witz nicht mehr so gut … Das ist die Arbeit eines Dichters. Der rechnet sich das Versmaß nicht mathematisch aus, sondern arbeitet nach seinem Gefühl" – eine treffende Analogie: Die ursprüngliche Bedeutung des Wortes *Poesie* ist „Erschaffung". Gedicht und Witz haben aber noch eine weitere Eigenschaft gemein, wenn sie gut gemacht sind: Sie sagen mit wenig viel.

Allen arbeitete sich von der Gagkomödie zur Psychokomödie hoch. *Der Stadtneurotiker*, *Manhattan* und *Hannah und ihre Schwestern* dringen in die tieferen Schichten des Humors vor, der auf Persönlichkeit beruht, und sie zeigen den Fortschritt des Künstlers seit *Was Sie schon immer über Sex wissen wollten** [*aber bisher nicht zu fragen wagten*], *Der Schläfer* und *Die letzte Nacht des Boris Gruschenko*. Ein gutes Beispiel dieser anspruchsvolleren Komik ist die Szene in *Der Stadtneurotiker*, in der die Leinwand geteilt ist und Annie und Alvy jeweils bei ihrem Psychiater sitzen. Auf die gleiche Frage, wie häufig sie Sex miteinander haben, antwortet Alvy: „Praktisch nie! Ich würde sagen, zwei- bis dreimal die Woche" und Annie: „Ständig! Ich würde sagen, zwei- bis dreimal die Woche." Diese „höhere" Komik (die George Meredith als „nachdenkliches Lachen" bezeichnete) bereichert die Emotion und unterstützt die Ernsthaftigkeit. Allens Werk offenbart auch die ergreifende Mischung der Tragikomödie in dem Charme und der Fantasie von *Purple Rose of Cairo*, der Nostalgie von *Radio Days*, den verschiedenen Handlungssträngen von *Verbrechen und andere Kleinigkeiten* (1989) und dem bittersüßen Ton von *Alice*.

Die jüngste Überraschung, die uns Allens *sprezzatura* beschert hat, ist die tragische Sicht von *Match Point*, seinem vollendetsten ernsthaften Film. Zu Allens Vorbildern zählen auch Eugene O'Neill und Ingmar Bergman, doch seine Ehrfurcht vor diesen Größen hemmte anfangs seine eigene Originalität. Sein dramatisches Werk (*Innenleben*, *September* und *Eine andere Frau*) erforderte eine längere Entwicklungsphase, bis sich auch hier die *sprezzatura* zeigte, die es locker erscheinen ließ. Allen selbst gestand Eric Lax gegenüber, dass er die Dialoge in *Innenleben* eher den formal-steifen Untertiteln von Bergman-Filmen entlehnt habe als dem gesprochenen Englisch. Der Erfolg von *Match Point* bei den Kritikern wie beim Publikum brachte Allen schließlich die lang ersehnte Wertschätzung, die man ihm bislang vorenthalten hatte: als Autor und Regisseur dramatischer Filme.

STILL FROM 'EVERYTHING YOU ALWAYS WANTED TO KNOW ABOUT SEX* (*BUT WERE AFRAID TO ASK)' (1972)

Reportedly, Woody never read the best seller on which his film is based but took the question/answer format to outrageous comic lengths. / Angeblich hatte Woody den Bestseller, auf dem der Film basiert, nie gelesen, aber er trieb das Frage-Antwort-Format auf hanebüchene Gipfel der Komik. / Woody Allen, qui prétend n'avoir jamais lu le best-seller dont s'inspire son film, pousse le format question/réponse jusqu'aux confins du loufoque.

WOODY ALLEN: L'ART DE LA FACÉTIE

Glenn Hopp

Le mot italien *sprezzatura* est difficile à définir. Il a été forgé par Baldassare Castiglione dans *Le Livre du courtisan* (1528) pour désigner ce don exquis propre à l'élite de la Renaissance, l'équivalent au XVIᵉ siècle des *beautiful people* de notre époque. Il décrit la nonchalance étudiée de ceux qui semblent accomplir sans effort les tâches les plus difficiles et réussir du premier jet les œuvres les plus travaillées. En ces temps voués au culte de la célébrité, la *sprezzatura* serait considérée comme un élément clé du charisme.

Ce n'est pas sans surprise que l'on découvre cette qualité en la personne de Woody Allen. Comment imaginer que derrière ce personnage comique, névrosé et gauche se cache un cinéaste consciencieux qui régit méticuleusement la moindre facette de ses films ? Avec ses airs de cocker abandonné, ce drôle de *schlemiel* (« empôté ») n'est pas sans rappeler le personnage de Charlot. Sa façon de parler et son humour fanfaron s'inspirent du style de Bob Hope, dont il idolâtre les films. Mais ce personnage cinématographique n'est qu'une des nombreuses œuvres que l'artiste Woody Allen a produites avec un naturel trompeur.

La première de ces œuvres fut sans doute un bon mot. Dès l'âge de 16 ans, le jeune Woody invente des mots d'esprit pour des chroniqueurs de journaux new-yorkais. Il ne tarde pas à écrire des blagues pour des humoristes et diverses émissions de télévision (avec l'aide inestimable de son mentor Danny, frère du scénariste Neil Simon). Enfin, Woody Allen se met à créer ses propres spectacles comiques, dont le succès lui permet de publier des articles dans *The New Yorker*, d'écrire deux comédies bien accueillies à Broadway et de réaliser ses premiers films truffés de gags. Mais déjà, l'artiste qui se

STILL FROM 'ANNIE HALL' (1977)
"I love your outfit," Alvy says to Annie. Her popular look was based on Diane Keaton's own style of dress. / „Mir gefällt dein Outfit", sagt Alvy zu Annie, deren populärer Kleidungsstil auf dem basierte, was Diane Keaton auch privat trug. / « J'adore votre tenue », déclare Alvy à Annie. Inspiré du style vestimentaire de Diane Keaton, le look d'Annie Hall est alors très en vogue.

« Le seul obstacle entre la grandeur et moi, c'est moi. »
Woody Allen en 2005

cache derrière la machine à blagues est conscient du travail nécessaire pour donner l'illusion de la facilité, comme il le confie à son biographe Eric Lax : « On exprime une pensée ou un sentiment sous une forme très condensée et tout repose sur le rythme des mots... Par exemple : "Je n'ai pas peur de mourir, mais je préfère ne pas être là quand ça arrivera..." Avec un mot de plus ou de moins, ça ne rendrait pas aussi bien... C'est ce que font les poètes. Ils ne comptent pas le nombre de pieds, ils le "sentent". » C'est une bonne analogie. Le sens étymologique du mot *poème* est « ouvrage, création ». Le poème et le mot d'esprit, s'ils sont bien faits, ont une autre définition commune : l'art d'en dire beaucoup en peu de mots.

Passant de la comédie burlesque à la comédie psychologique, Woody Allen abandonne les sketches parodiques de *Tout ce que vous avez toujours voulu savoir sur le sexe*, *Woody et les robots* et *Guerre et Amour* pour l'humour plus raffiné de *Annie Hall*, *Manhattan* et *Hannah et ses sœurs*. La scène en écran partagé de *Annie Hall* où Annie et Alvy apparaissent simultanément, chacun lors d'une séance chez son psy, offre une bonne illustration de cet humour fondé sur la psychologie des personnages. Interrogés sur la fréquence à laquelle ils font l'amour, Alvy répond : « Presque jamais ! Seulement deux ou trois fois par semaine », tandis qu'Annie s'exclame : « Constamment ! Au moins deux ou trois fois par semaine. » Cet humour sophistiqué (que George Meredith qualifie de « rire cérébral ») enrichit les émotions et incite à la réflexion. Woody Allen maîtrise également le poignant mélange des genres propre à la tragi-comédie, comme le prouvent le charme et la fantaisie de *La Rose pourpre du Caire*, la nostalgie de *Radio Days*, les intrigues entremêlées de *Crimes et délits* et le ton doux-amer d'*Alice*.

La dernière illustration en date de la *sprezzatura* de Woody Allen est la noirceur de *Match Point*, le plus accompli de ses films dramatiques. Si le cinéaste compte parmi ses idoles des artistes graves comme Eugene O'Neill et Ingmar Bergman, la vénération qu'il leur voue a sans doute étouffé sa créativité à ses débuts. Ses œuvres dramatiques (*Intérieurs*, *September*, *Une autre femme*) ont nécessité une plus longue évolution avant de parvenir à donner l'illusion du naturel. Comme il l'a lui-même reconnu dans un recueil d'entretiens avec Eric Lax, les dialogues d'*Intérieurs* relèvent plus des sous-titres guindés des films de Bergman que de l'anglais idiomatique. Mais aujourd'hui, grâce au succès critique et commercial de *Match Point*, Woody Allen est enfin reconnu et respecté en tant qu'auteur et réalisateur dramatique.

STILL FROM 'ANNIE HALL' (1977)
Woody Allen's most honored film, a winner for best actress, director, script, and film at both the Oscars and BAFTA. / Woody Allens Film mit den meisten Auszeichnungen: Er gewann sowohl den amerikanischen „Oscar" als auch den britischen „BAFTA Award" für die beste Darstellerin in einer Hauptrolle, die beste Regie, das beste Drehbuch und den besten Film. / L'œuvre la plus récompensée de Woody Allen, avec les prix du Meilleur film, du Meilleur scénario, de la Meilleure mise en scène et de la Meilleure actrice à la fois aux Oscars et aux BAFTA Awards.

PAGE 22
PORTRAIT (1961)
The successful, if neurotic, stand-up comic, circa 1961. Larry Gelbart called him "a tadpole in horn-rims." / Der erfolgreiche, wenn auch neurotische Stand-up-Comedian um 1961. Larry Gelbart nannte ihn eine „Kaulquappe mit Hornbrille". / Un artiste de stand-up dont les névroses n'empêchent pas le succès, vers 1961. Larry Gelbart l'a qualifié de « têtard à lunettes d'écaille ».

2

VISUAL FILMOGRAPHY

FILMOGRAFIE IN BILDERN

FILMOGRAPHIE EN IMAGES

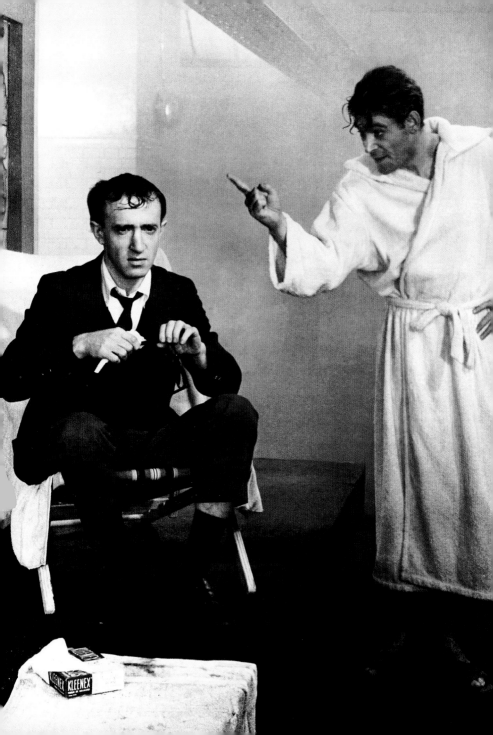

ON THE SET OF 'WHAT'S NEW PUSSYCAT?' (1965)
With the cast, including Peter Sellers and Peter O'Toole at right. The film title quotes Warren Beatty's way of answering his telephone. / Mit den Schauspielkollegen, darunter Peter Sellers und Peter O'Toole (rechts). Der Filmtitel zitiert den Satz, mit dem Warren Beatty seine Telefongespräche annahm. / Woody et ses acteurs, dont Peter Sellers et Peter O'Toole (à droite). Le titre du film reprend la formule utilisée par Warren Beatty lorsqu'il répond au téléphone.

STILL FROM 'WHAT'S NEW PUSSYCAT?' (1965)
With Peter O'Toole. The film was a big-budget success, but the lack of creative control made Woody wary of the Hollywood system. / Mit Peter O'Toole. Der mit hohem Budget gedrehte Film war ein Kassenschlager, doch der Mangel an kreativem Einfluss weckte Allens Argwohn gegenüber dem Hollywoodsystem. / Aux côtés de Peter O'Toole. Malgré le succès commercial de ce film à gros budget, le manque de liberté artistique rend Woody Allen méfiant à l'égard du système hollywoodien.

ON THE SET OF 'WHAT'S NEW PUSSYCAT?' (1965)

The many script rewrites called for by producer Charles K. Feldman seem to have taken their toll on writer-performer Woody. / Es scheint, dass die zahlreichen Drehbuchänderungen, die Produzent Charles K. Feldman forderte, ihre Spuren bei Drehbuchautor und Darsteller Allen hinterließen. / Les nombreux remaniements du scénario exigés par le producteur Charles K. Feldman semblent avoir épuisé l'acteur-scénariste Woody Allen.

"I'm a serious person, a disciplined worker, interested in writing, interested in literature, interested in theater and film. I'm not so inept as I depict myself for comic purposes."
Woody Allen

„Ich bin ein ernster Mensch, ein disziplinierter Arbeiter, der sich für das Schreiben interessiert, für Literatur, für Theater und Film. Ich bin keineswegs so unbeholfen, wie ich mich zu komödiantischen Zwecken darstelle."
Woody Allen

« Je suis quelqu'un de sérieux, un travailleur discipliné, qui s'intéresse à l'écriture, à la littérature, au théâtre et au cinéma. Je ne suis pas aussi incompétent que je prétends l'être à des fins comiques. »
Woody Allen

**ON THE SET OF 'WHAT'S NEW PUSSYCAT?'
(1965)**
Director Clive Donner gives instruction to an
uninspired-looking Woody Allen. / Regisseur Clive
Donner gibt einem lustlos wirkenden Woody Allen
Regieanweisungen. / Le coréalisateur Clive Donner
donne ses instructions à un Woody Allen apparemment
en mal d'inspiration.

STILL FROM 'WHAT'S UP, TIGER LILY?' (1966)
Spies seek an egg-salad recipe in this silly film in which
Woody dubbed and synched a new soundtrack to a
Japanese B-movie. / In dieser Farce, bei der Woody
Allen einer japanischen Billigproduktion eine bewusst
alberne Synchronisation verpasst hatte, suchen Spione
nach einem Rezept für Eiersalat. / Des espions à la
recherche d'une recette d'œufs mayonnaise dans ce
film saugrenu, monté à partir d'une série B japonaise
dont Woody Allen réécrit et réenregistre les dialogues.

*"His previous writing credit, I assumed, must have
been learning the alphabet. He seemed so fragile,
a tadpole in horn-rims."*
Writer Larry Gelbart on first meeting the young
Woody Allen

*„Ich dachte, sein bisheriger schriftstellerischer
Verdienst sei das Lernen des Alphabets gewesen.
Er schien so zerbrechlich – eine Kaulquappe mit
Hornbrille.“*
Autor Larry Gelbart über seine erste Begegnung mit dem
jungen Woody Allen

*« À le voir, on aurait dit que son expérience en
matière d'écriture s'était limitée à l'apprentissage
de l'alphabet. Il semblait si fragile, un têtard à
lunettes d'écaille. »*
Le scénariste Larry Gelbart au sujet de sa première
rencontre avec le jeune Woody Allen

POSTER FOR 'WHAT'S UP, TIGER LILY?' (1966)
Comma or no comma? Print references to the film usually include it, but the poster art omits it creating bawdy innuendo. / Mit oder ohne Komma? In gedruckten Texten wird es meist gesetzt, aber auf dem Poster fehlt es – wodurch der Titel eine ziemlich obszöne Zweideutigkeit erhält. / L'affiche originale du film, où l'omission de la virgule confère au titre une ambiguïté salace (« Quoi de neuf, Lily la tigresse ? » devient « Qu'est-ce qui grimpe sur Lily la tigresse ? »).

"What [audiences] want is an intimacy with the person. They want to like the person and find the person funny as a human being. The biggest trap comedians fall into is trying to get by on the basis of their material. That's just hiding behind jokes."
Woody Allen on stand-up comedy

„Was [das Publikum] möchte, ist eine Vertrautheit mit der Person. Sie wollen die Person mögen und als Menschen lustig finden. Die größte Falle für einen Comedian ist, wenn er denkt, er schaffe es allein auf der Grundlage seines Materials. Dann versteckt er sich nur hinter seinen Witzen."
Woody Allen über Stand-up-Comedy

« Ce que veut [le public], c'est l'intimité avec la personne. Il veut vous aimer et vous trouver drôle en tant qu'être humain. Le plus gros piège dans lequel tombent les comiques, c'est de se reposer sur leurs sketches. Ils ne font dès lors que se cacher derrière leurs blagues. »
Woody Allen au sujet de l'art du stand-up

STILL FROM 'CASINO ROYALE' (1967)
Ten writers and six directors, credited and uncredited, make for a clumsy, cumbersome spoof of Bond movies. / Zehn Autoren und sechs Regisseure – von denen einige nicht einmal namentlich erwähnt wurden – rührten eine plumpe und schwerfällige Parodie auf die James-Bond-Filme zusammen. / La présence de dix scénaristes et six réalisateurs, mentionnés ou non au générique, explique la maladresse et la lourdeur de cette parodie des films de James Bond.

ON THE SET OF 'TAKE THE MONEY AND RUN' (1969)

Filming began in San Quentin prison. Woody was so nervous that reportedly he cut himself shaving that morning. / Die Dreharbeiten begannen im Gefängnis von San Quentin. Allen war so nervös, dass er sich angeblich an diesem Morgen beim Rasieren verletzte. / Paniqué par le tournage à la prison de San Quentin, Woody se serait coupé en se rasant le matin du premier jour.

"I talked with Arthur Penn before I shot Take the Money [and Run]. But I read very little about filmmaking. I have no technical background even to this day. It's a mystique promulgated by the film industry that technical background is a big deal. You can learn about cameras and lighting very quickly."
Woody Allen in 1973

„Ich sprach mit Arthur Penn, bevor ich Woody, der Unglücksrabe drehte. Aber ich hatte sehr wenig über das Filmemachen gelesen. Selbst heute noch besitze ich keinerlei technisches Hintergrundwissen. Es gehört zu den Mythen, die von der Filmindustrie verbreitet werden, dass technisches Hintergrundwissen eine große Sache ist. Dabei kann man sehr schnell etwas über Kameras und Ausleuchtung lernen."
Woody Allen 1973

**STILL FROM 'TAKE THE MONEY AND RUN'
(1969)**
Sight gag in the prison laundry. / Ein optischer Gag in der
Wäscherei des Männergefängnisses. / Gag visuel dans la
laverie de la prison.

*« J'ai parlé avec Arthur Penn avant de tourner
Prends l'oseille [et tire-toi]. Mais j'ai très peu
étudié les techniques de tournage. Aujourd'hui
encore, je n'ai aucune formation technique.
C'est un mythe propagé par l'industrie
cinématographique qui veut que la formation
technique soit toute une affaire. On peut
apprendre à maîtriser la caméra et l'éclairage
très rapidement. »*
Woody Allen en 1973

**STILL FROM 'TAKE THE MONEY AND RUN'
(1969)**
With love interest Janet Margolin, who also appears
briefly in 'Annie Hall', as Alvy's second wife. / Die
Freundin spielt hier Janet Margolin, die auch in
Der Stadtneurotiker kurz als Alvys zweite Ehefrau zu
sehen ist. / Avec son flirt, Janet Margolin, qui apparaît
brièvement dans *Annie Hall* dans le rôle de la seconde
épouse d'Alvy.

**STILL FROM 'TAKE THE MONEY AND RUN'
(1969)**
The film's mock-documentary form is broader in its
comedy than the more accomplished 'Zelig' (1983). /
Der pseudodokumentarische Stil des Films ist in seiner
Komik gröber gestrickt als der raffinierter angelegte
Zelig (1983). / Avec son style pseudo-documentaire, ce
film est une comédie moins subtile que *Zelig* (1983),
œuvre plus accomplie.

STILL FROM 'BANANAS' (1971)
Woody teaches a revolutionary how to shave. / Fielding (Allen) bringt einem Revoluzzer das Rasieren bei. / Woody apprend à un révolutionnaire à se raser.

PORTRAIT FOR 'BANANAS' (1971)
Televised assassination, Howard Cosell in the bedroom, naked women in the jungle—all part of the zany world of early Allen comedy. / Ein politischer Mord, der live im Fernsehen übertragen wird, Sportreporter Howard Cosell im Schlafzimmer während einer Hochzeitsnacht, barbusige Frauen im Dschungel - all das sind Bestandteile der verrückten Welt einer frühen Allen-Komödie. / Le célèbre reporter sportif Howard Cosell commentant un assassinat en direct à la télévision, retransmission en direct d'une nuit de noces, femmes nues dans la jungle : tous les ingrédients de l'univers loufoque des premières comédies de Woody Allen.

STILL FROM 'BANANAS' (1971)
The Woody Allen outsider becomes a revolutionary,
then the president of San Marcos, a fictional South
American republic. / Der von Woody Allen dargestellte
Außenseiter wird erst zum Revoluzzer und dann sogar
zum Präsidenten der fiktiven Bananenrepublik San
Marcos. / Devenu révolutionnaire, le timide Woody
Allen se retrouve président de San Marcos, république
fictive d'Amérique du Sud.

STILL FROM 'BANANAS' (1971)
Woody plays Fielding Mellish, a product tester. / Woody
Allen spielt den Warentester Fielding Mellish. / Woody
incarne Fielding Mellish, testeur de produits.

STILL FROM 'PLAY IT AGAIN, SAM' (1972)
Based on Allen's Broadway play and written by him for
the screen, the film was directed by Herbert Ross. /
Herbert Ross führte Regie bei diesem Film, der auf
Allens Broadway-Stück basiert und für den Allen auch
das Drehbuch verfasst hatte. / Tiré de la pièce de
Woody Allen, qu'il a lui-même adaptée à l'écran, ce film
est réalisé par Herbert Ross.

STILL FROM 'PLAY IT AGAIN, SAM' (1972)
Allan Felix (Woody Allen), here with Linda Christie
(Diane Keaton), idolizes Humphrey Bogart and is
dwarfed by him in his imagination and in the bedroom. /
Allan Felix (Woody Allen), hier mit Linda Christie (Diane
Keaton), vergöttert Humphrey Bogart und schrumpft in
dessen Gegenwart zum Zwerg – sowohl in seiner
Fantasie als auch im Schlafzimmer. / Allan Felix (Woody
Allen), ici avec Linda Christie (Diane Keaton), idolâtre
Humphrey Bogart dont la grandeur le rapetisse, au
propre comme au figuré.

**STILL FROM 'EVERYTHING YOU ALWAYS
WANTED TO KNOW ABOUT SEX* (*BUT WERE
AFRAID TO ASK)' (1972)**
Gene Wilder and a sheep named Daisy answer the
question "What Is Sodomy?" / Gene Wilder und ein
Schaf namens Daisy beantworten die Frage: „Was ist
Sodomie?" / Gene Wilder et une brebis nommée Daisy
répondent à la question : « Qu'est-ce que la sodomie ? »

**STILL FROM 'EVERYTHING YOU ALWAYS
WANTED TO KNOW ABOUT SEX* (*BUT WERE
AFRAID TO ASK)' (1972)**
"What Happens During Ejaculation?" Woody as a sperm
who waits for instructions from Emission Control. /
„Was geschieht beim Samenerguss?" Woody Allen spielt
ein Spermium, das auf den Einsatzbefehl aus der
Ergusszentrale („Emission Control") wartet. / Woody en
spermatozoïde attendant son ordre d'évacuation dans
le sketch « Qu'est-ce qui advient durant une
éjaculation ? »

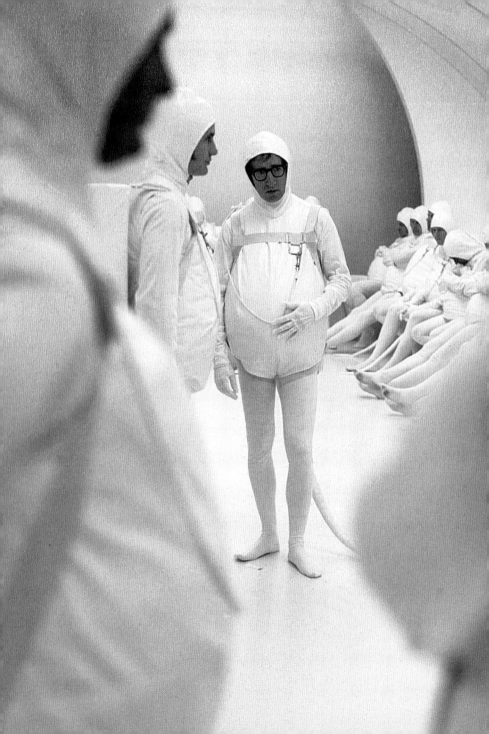

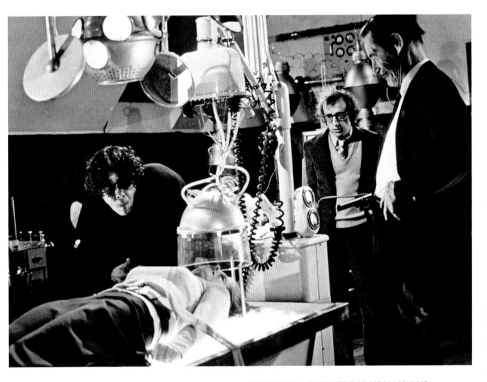

STILL FROM 'EVERYTHING YOU ALWAYS WANTED TO KNOW ABOUT SEX* (*BUT WERE AFRAID TO ASK)' (1972)
John Carradine (right) plays the mad scientist. / John Carradine (rechts) spielt den verrückten Wissenschaftler. / John Carradine (à droite) dans le rôle du savant fou.

ON THE SET OF 'EVERYTHING YOU ALWAYS WANTED TO KNOW ABOUT SEX* (*BUT WERE AFRAID TO ASK)' (1972)
The mad-scientist parody features a 40-foot runaway breast that must be lured into a giant bra. / In der Parodie auf verrückte Wissenschaftler ist eine zwölf Meter große „entflohene" Brust zu sehen, die mit einem passenden Riesen-BH wieder eingefangen werden muss. / Tentative de capture d'un gigantesque sein échappé d'un laboratoire lors d'une expérience scientifique hasardeuse.

STILL FROM 'EVERYTHING YOU ALWAYS WANTED TO KNOW ABOUT SEX* (*BUT WERE AFRAID TO ASK)' (1972)
David Reuben, author of the best seller, called the film "a sexual tragedy. Every episode in the picture was a chronicle of failure, which was the converse of everything in the book." / David Reuben, der Verfasser des Sachbuchbestsellers, nannte den Film „eine sexuelle Tragödie. Jede Episode des Films war eine Chronik des Misslingens und damit das Gegenteil von allem im Buch". / David Reuben, auteur du best-seller, qualifie le film de « tragédie sexuelle ». « Chaque épisode est la chronique d'un échec, ce qui est en parfaite contradiction avec le livre. »

ON THE SET OF 'EVERYTHING YOU ALWAYS WANTED TO KNOW ABOUT SEX* (*BUT WERE AFRAID TO ASK)' (1972)
This sequence, with Louise Lasser as a black-widow spider and Woody as her mate/main course, was cut from the film. / Diese Sequenz – mit Louise Lasser als Schwarze Witwe und Woody Allen als Spinnenmännchen und zugleich Mahlzeit – wurde aus dem Film herausgeschnitten. / Cette scène, avec Louise Lasser en veuve noire ne faisant qu'une bouchée de son amant (Woody Allen), a été coupée au montage.

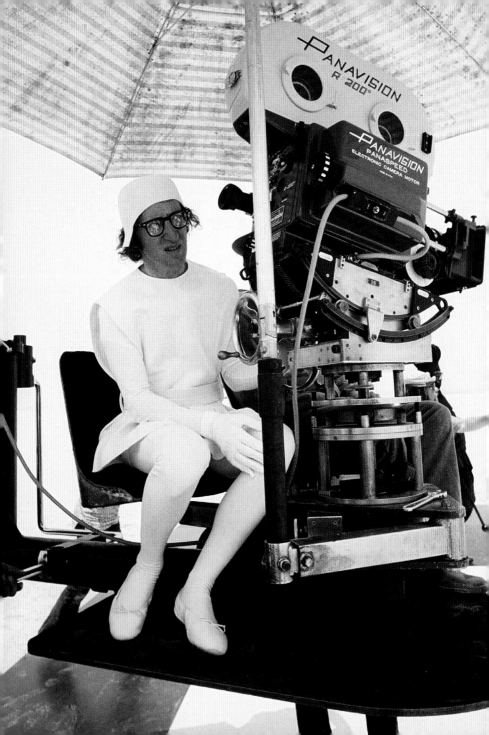

STILL FROM 'SLEEPER' (1973)
Miles Monroe finds something he likes in this dystopian future. / In dieser dystopischen Zukunft findet Miles Monroe etwas, das ihm gefällt. / Miles Monroe trouve quand même de quoi se réjouir dans ce futur dystopique.

ON THE SET OF 'SLEEPER' (1973)
Woody's character, Miles Monroe, is frozen after surgical complications in 1973 and unthawed in 2173. / Woody Allens Filmfigur Miles Monroe wird nach Komplikationen bei einem chirurgischen Eingriff 1973 eingefroren und 2173 wieder aufgetaut. / Miles Monroe, le personnage de Woody, a été congelé en 1973 à la suite de complications chirurgicales et décongelé en 2173.

ON THE SET OF 'SLEEPER' (1973)
In costume as the robot-valet with Diane Keaton. /
Kostümiert als Roboterdiener mit Diane Keaton. /
Aux côtés de Diane Keaton dans son costume de
robot-valet.

"There's no question that comedy's harder to do
than serious stuff. There's also no question in my
mind that comedy is less valuable than serious
stuff."
Woody Allen in 1972

„Es steht außer Frage, dass Komödie schwerer ist
als ernstes Zeug. Für mich steht aber auch außer
Frage, dass Komödie weniger wertvoll ist als
ernstes Zeug."
Woody Allen 1972

« Il ne fait aucun doute que la comédie est plus
difficile que les sujets sérieux. Mais il ne fait
également aucun doute dans mon esprit que la
comédie a moins de valeur que les sujets sérieux. »
Woody Allen en 1972

STILL FROM 'SLEEPER' (1973)
The outrageousness of the early comedies has led some
critics to fault Woody's sense of structure. / Allens
frühe Komödien waren so hanebüchen, dass ihm einige
Kritiker vorwarfen, ihm fehle der Sinn für eine
strukturierte Handlung. / L'extravagance des premières
comédies de Woody Allen conduit certains critiques à
mettre en doute son sens de la structure.

"I do think the salient feature about human existence is man's inhumanity to man. If you were looking at it from a distance, you know, if we were being observed by space people, I think that's what you would come away with. I don't think they'd be amazed by our art or by how much we've accomplished. I think they'd be sort of awestruck by the carnage and stupidity."
Woody Allen in 1988

„Ich glaube, das hervorstechende Merkmal des menschlichen Daseins ist die Unmenschlichkeit des Menschen gegenüber dem Menschen. Wenn man es aus der Entfernung betrachtete, wissen Sie, so als ob wir von Weltraumwesen beobachtet würden, dann wäre das Ihr Eindruck, denke ich. Ich glaube nicht, dass sie unsere Kunst bestaunen würden oder das, was wir erreicht haben. Ich denke, sie wären irgendwie baff angesichts des Gemetzels und der Blödheit."
Woody Allen 1988

« Je pense que le trait le plus marquant de la condition humaine est l'inhumanité de l'homme envers l'homme. Si on regardait cela de loin, si on était observés par des extraterrestres, c'est sûrement ce qui ressortirait. Je ne pense pas qu'ils seraient ébahis par notre art ou par tout ce que nous avons accompli. Je crois qu'ils seraient abasourdis par tant de carnages et de stupidité. »
Woody Allen en 1988

STILL FROM 'LOVE AND DEATH' (1975)
A broadly comic epic, the film satirizes Russian literature, among other topics. / Als komisches Epos mit teilweise grobem Humor zieht der Film unter anderem die russische Literatur durch den Kakao. / Cette comédie burlesque parodie notamment les épopées de la littérature russe.

STILL FROM 'LOVE AND DEATH' (1975)
Woody and actor Harold Gould in a duelling scene.
The film was made in Paris and Budapest. / Woody
Allen und Harold Gould in einer Duellszene. Der Film
wurde in Paris und Budapest gedreht. / Scène de duel
entre Woody Allen et Harold Gould dans ce film tourné
à Paris et à Budapest.

"Years ago Paddy Chayefsky said to me, 'When a
movie is failing or a play is failing'—he put it so
brilliantly—'cut out the wisdom.' ... Marshall
Brickman said it a different way ... but just as
cogently and insightful: 'The message of the film
can't be in the dialogue.'"
Woody Allen in 2006

„Vor Jahren sagte Paddy Chayefsky zu mir: ‚Wenn
ein Film misslingt oder ein Theaterstück misslingt'
- er hat es so herrlich formuliert -, ‚dann nimm die
Weisheit raus.' ... Marshall Brickman drückte es
anders aus ... aber ebenso überzeugend und
aufschlussreich: ‚Die Botschaft eines Films darf
nicht in den Dialogen stecken.'"
Woody Allen 2006

STILL FROM 'LOVE AND DEATH' (1975)
What is death like? "You know the chicken at Tresky's Restaurant? It's worse." / Wie ist der Tod? „Kennst du das Hühnchen in Tresky's Restaurant? Er ist noch schlimmer!" / Comment c'est, la mort ? « Tu te souviens du poulet chez Tresky ? C'est pire. »

« Il y a des années, Paddy Chayefsky a eu cette formule merveilleuse : "Quand un film ou une pièce ne fonctionne pas, enlevez la sagesse." [...] Marshall Brickman l'a formulé différemment, mais de façon tout aussi pertinente : "Le message d'un film ne peut résider dans les dialogues."»
Woody Allen en 2006

STILL FROM 'THE FRONT' (1976)
Woody plays a front for blacklisted writers in McCarthy-era America. The film was written by Walter Bernstein and directed by Martin Ritt, both of whom were blacklisted. / Woody Allen spielt einen Strohmann für Autoren, die im Amerika der McCarthy-Ära auf der Schwarzen Liste stehen. Sowohl Drehbuchautor Walter Bernstein als auch Regisseur Martin Ritt kannten dies aus eigener Erfahrung. / À l'époque du maccarthysme, Woody sert de prête-nom à des auteurs placés sur liste noire dans ce film du scénariste Walter Bernstein et du réalisateur Martin Ritt, tous deux victimes de la chasse aux sorcières.

"My fear that I wouldn't have courage under the right circumstances always humiliates me when I'm alone with myself. I cannot think of an act I've done that required courage of any significance."
Woody Allen, *Woody Allen: A Biography* by Eric Lax

„Meine Angst, dass ich unter den richtigen Umständen keinen Mut haben würde, scheint mir immer demütigend, wenn ich mit mir allein bin. Ich kann mich an keine Situation erinnern, die nennenswerten Mut erfordert hätte."
Woody Allen, *Woody Allen: Eine Biographie* von Eric Lax

STILL FROM 'THE FRONT' (1976)
The tragic story of Hecky Brown, played by Zero Mostel, himself a blacklisted actor in the 1950s, is the most compelling part of the film. / Das Eindringlichste an diesem Film ist die tragische Geschichte von Hecky Brown, gespielt von Zero Mostel, der in den 1950er-Jahren als Schauspieler selbst auf der Schwarzen Liste stand. / L'élément le plus captivant de l'histoire est le sort tragique de Hecky Brown, incarné par Zero Mostel, qui fut lui-même placé sur liste noire dans les années 1950.

« La crainte de ne pas avoir le courage nécessaire si les circonstances l'exigeaient est une constante humiliation intérieure. Je ne me souviens pas d'avoir commis un seul acte qui nécessite un tant soit peu de courage. »
Woody Allen, *Woody Allen: A Biography* d'Eric Lax

STILL FROM 'ANNIE HALL' (1977)
Woody as Alvy Singer in what is probably his most memorable role. / Woody Allen als Alvy Singer in seiner wahrscheinlich denkwürdigsten Rolle. / Woody dans le rôle d'Alvy Singer, sans doute le plus mémorable de sa carrière.

STILL FROM 'ANNIE HALL' (1977)
"I hate gadgets—cameras, tape recorders, airplanes. There are certain things in life that you're not just indifferent to, they're actually offputting."—Woody Allen to biographer Eric Lax / „Ich hasse Technik - Kameras, Tonbandgeräte, Flugzeuge. Es gibt bestimmte Dinge im Leben, denen gegenüber man nicht einfach nur gleichgültig ist - sie ekeln einen wirklich an." — Woody Allen zu seinem Biografen Eric Lax / « Je déteste les gadgets, les appareils photo, les magnétophones, les avions. Il y a des choses qui ne nous sont pas seulement indifférentes, mais qui nous font franchement horreur. » — Woody Allen à son biographe Eric Lax

DINO DE LAURENTIIS PRESENTS
INGMAR BERGMAN'S
"FACE TO FACE"
Starring
LIV ULLMANN
Directed and Produced by INGMAR BERGMAN Filmed in Color
A Paramount Release

STILL FROM 'ANNIE HALL' (1977)
The characters visit their psychiatrists, revealing their differing views on the same subjects. Analysis has been a recurrent subject for Woody's comedy since his stand-up days. / Die Figuren besuchen ihre jeweiligen Psychiater und geben dabei ihre unterschiedlichen Ansichten zu den gleichen Dingen preis. Die Psychoanalyse ist in Allens Arbeit ein wiederkehrendes Thema, schon seit seinen Tagen als Stand-up-Komiker. / Les protagonistes rendent visite à leurs psy, révélant ainsi leurs divergences de vues sur des sujets communs. La psychanalyse est un thème récurrent chez Woody Allen depuis ses débuts dans le registre du stand-up.

PAGES 60/61
STILL FROM 'ANNIE HALL' (1977)
"[Diane Keaton] knows me for the schlemiel I am."— Woody Allen to Eric Lax (2006) / „[Diane Keaton] weiß, was für ein Schlemihl ich bin." — Woody Allen zu Eric Lax (2006) / « [Diane Keaton] sait quel empoté je suis. » — Woody Allen à Eric Lax (2006)

STILL FROM 'ANNIE HALL' (1977)
The lofty chat of Annie and Alvy is undercut by subtitles of what they're thinking: 'I wonder what she looks like naked?' / Die abgehobene Konversation zwischen Annie und Alvy wird von Untertiteln entlarvt, die ihre unausgesprochenen Gedanken enthüllen: „Ich frage mich, wie sie wohl nackt aussieht." / Les propos intello échangés par Annie et Alvy sont contredits par les sous-titres qui trahissent leurs pensées: « Et à poil, comment est-elle ? »

"Annie Hall was a much-adored picture. I mean, it's fine, but I've done better pictures than that, though it may have had a warmth, an emotion that people responded to."
Woody Allen in 2005

„Der Stadtneurotiker war ein Film, der sehr bewundert wurde. Ich meine, er ist nett, aber ich habe bessere Filme als diesen gemacht, wenngleich er eine Wärme besaß, eine Emotion, auf die die Leute ansprachen."
Woody Allen 2005

« Le public a adoré Annie Hall. C'est un bon film, mais j'en ai fait de meilleurs, même s'il possède sans doute une chaleur, une qualité émotionnelle qui a touché les spectateurs. »
Woody Allen en 2005

ON THE SET OF 'INTERIORS' (1978)
The director with Geraldine Page, who plays Eve, an artist who controls her family and their environment. / Der Regisseur mit Geraldine Page in der Rolle der Eve, einer Künstlerin, die ihre Familie und ihre Umgebung kontrolliert. / Le metteur en scène avec Geraldine Page dans le rôle d'Eve, une artiste qui cherche à tout contrôler autour d'elle.

STILL FROM 'INTERIORS' (1978)
Woody Allen's first dramatic film is influenced by the work of Ingmar Bergman and Eugene O'Neill. / Woody Allens erstes Filmdrama ist von den Werken Ingmar Bergmans und Eugene O'Neills beeinflusst. / Le premier film dramatique de Woody Allen est influencé par l'œuvre d'Ingmar Bergman et d'Eugene O'Neill.

STILL FROM 'INTERIORS' (1978)
The film's three sisters, played by Diane Keaton, Kristin
Griffith, and Mary Beth Hurt, each try to be themselves
without hurting their mother. / Jede der drei Schwestern
des Films - gespielt von Diane Keaton, Kristin Griffith
und Mary Beth Hurt - versucht, sich selbst zu
verwirklichen, ohne die Mutter zu verletzen. / Les trois
sœurs, interprétées par Diane Keaton, Kristin Griffith et
Mary Beth Hurt, tentent d'assumer leur identité sans
contrarier leur mère.

"I felt in my mind, hopefully this [early success with
Take the Money and Run and Bananas] would be a
stepping-stone to more serious things that I enjoy
more. Because I myself—and I'm going only as a
viewer—enjoy more serious things."
Woody Allen in 2005

„Ich hatte die Vorstellung in meinem Kopf, dass
[der frühe Erfolg mit Woody, der Unglücksrabe
und Bananas] hoffentlich ein Sprungbrett sein
würde für die ernsthafteren Dinge, die mir mehr
Spaß machen. Denn ich selbst - und das sage ich
jetzt ausschließlich als Zuschauer - mag die
ernsteren Dinge."
Woody Allen 2005

STILL FROM 'INTERIORS' (1978)

"Those three dramas—'Interiors', 'September', and 'Another Woman'—were very ambitious. So when I struck out, it was apparent and egregious and not entertaining."—Woody Allen to Eric Lax (2006) / „Diese drei Dramen - *Innenleben, September* und *Eine andere Frau* - waren sehr ehrgeizig. Wenn ich also einen Misserfolg hatte, dann war es offensichtlich und ungeheuerlich und nicht unterhaltsam." — Woody Allen zu Eric Lax (2006) / « Ces trois drames - *Intérieurs, September* et *Une autre femme* - étaient très ambitieux. Alors quand je me suis planté, c'était flagrant et pas très distrayant. » — Woody Allen à Eric Lax (2006)

« En mon for intérieur, j'espérais que ce [premier succès avec Prends l'oseille et tire-toi et Bananas] serait un tremplin vers des choses plus sérieuses qui me plaisent plus. Car moi - je parle en tant que spectateur -, j'aime mieux les films sérieux. »
Woody Allen en 2005

STILL FROM 'MANHATTAN' (1979)
Isaac Davis (Woody Allen) spends time with his best
friend's mistress, Mary Wilkie (Diane Keaton), in Central
Park. Critic Andrew Sarris called 'Manhattan' "the only
truly great film of the '70s." / Isaac Davis (Woody Allen)
verbringt einige Zeit mit Mary Wilkie (Diane Keaton),
der Geliebten seines besten Freundes, im New Yorker
Central Park. Kritiker Andrew Sarris nannte *Manhattan*
„den einzigen wirklich großen Film der Siebziger". /
Isaac Davis (Woody Allen) dans Central Park avec la
maîtresse de son meilleur ami, Mary Wilkie (Diane
Keaton). Selon le critique Andrew Sarris, *Manhattan*
« est le seul grand film des années 70 ».

*"No one sees that the New York I show [in movies]
is the New York I know only from Hollywood films
that I grew up on—penthouses, white telephones,
beautiful streets, waterfronts, going through
Central Park on carriage rides."*
Woody Allen in 2006

*„Keiner sieht, dass das New York, das ich [in
Filmen] zeige, das New York ist, das ich nur aus
den Hollywoodfilmen kenne, mit denen ich
aufwuchs - Penthouse-Wohnungen, weiße
Telefone, schöne Straßen, Uferpromenaden,
Kutschfahrten durch den Central Park."*
Woody Allen 2006

STILL FROM 'MANHATTAN' (1979)
Isaac and Mary disagree about everything, especially about the arts. / Isaac und Mary sind in allem unterschiedlicher Meinung, insbesondere in Sachen Kunst. / Isaac et Mary sont en désaccord sur tout, notamment en matière d'art.

« Personne ne voit que le New York que je montre [dans mes films] est le New York du cinéma hollywoodien avec lequel j'ai grandi : les lofts, les téléphones blancs, les avenues élégantes, les fronts de mer, les promenades en calèche dans Central Park. »
Woody Allen en 2006

PAGES 70/71
STILL FROM 'MANHATTAN' (1979)
Gordon Willis's black-and-white photography gives the film its distinctive look. / Die Schwarz-Weiß-Bilder von Gordon Willis geben dem Film seinen unverwechselbaren Look. / La photographie en noir et blanc de Gordon Willis confère au film un style particulier.

STILL FROM 'MANHATTAN' (1979)
Isaac's wife, Jill (Meryl Streep), left him for another
woman and is writing a book about it. / Isaacs Ehefrau
Jill (Meryl Streep) verließ ihn, um mit einer Frau
zusammenzuziehen, und schreibt nun ein Buch
darüber. / La femme d'Isaac, Jill (Meryl Streep), l'a
quitté pour aller vivre auprès d'une autre femme et
écrit un livre à ce sujet.

"Basically, I shoot the script. I like to get a first
draft on film and then see where I am. I discover
radical things I never would know otherwise.
A script is only a guide for the work to come."
Woody Allen in 1987

„Im Grunde verfilme ich zunächst das Drehbuch.
Ich hab gerne einen ersten Entwurf auf Film und
schau mir dann an, wo ich stehe. Ich entdecke
dabei fundamentale Dinge, die mir sonst entgehen
würden. Ein Drehbuch ist nur ein Leitfaden für die
Arbeit, die dann folgt."
Woody Allen 1987

« Pour commencer, je filme le scénario. J'aime avoir
un premier jet sur la pellicule pour voir où j'en suis.
Je découvre des choses fondamentales que je
n'aurais jamais vues autrement. Le scénario n'est
qu'une trame pour le travail à venir. »
Woody Allen en 1987

STILL FROM 'MANHATTAN' (1979)
17-year-old Tracy (Mariel Hemingway) is probably the
most mature character in the film. She tells Isaac to
have more faith in people. / Die 17-jährige Tracy
(Mariel Hemingway) ist vermutlich die reifste Figur des
Films. Sie ermuntert Isaac, mehr an die Menschen zu
glauben. / Du haut de ses 17 ans, Tracy (Mariel
Hemingway) est sans doute le personnage le plus mûr
du film. Elle conseille à Isaac d'avoir foi en son prochain.

"The point of the story [of Stardust Memories] is that he [the protagonist] can't get used to the fact that he's mortal and that all his wealth and fame and adulation are not going to preserve him in any meaningful way—he too will age and die."
Woody Allen in 2005

„Der Kern der Handlung [von Stardust Memories] ist, dass [der Protagonist] sich nicht damit abfinden kann, dass er sterblich ist und dass all sein Ruhm und all sein Reichtum und alle Lobhudelei ihn nicht auf irgendeine sinnvolle Weise erhalten können - er wird altern und sterben."
Woody Allen 2005

« Le nœud de l'histoire [de Stardust Memories] est que [le héros] ne peut se faire à l'idée qu'il est mortel et que toute sa fortune, sa célébrité et l'adulation dont il fait l'objet ne le protégeront pas de l'essentiel, que lui aussi va vieillir et mourir. »
Woody Allen en 2005

STILL FROM 'STARDUST MEMORIES' (1980)
Former comedy filmmaker Sandy Bates (Allen) romances Daisy (Jessica Harper) in an attempt to recapture his lost love for Dorrie. / Sandy Bates (Allen), ein Filmemacher, der einstmals Komödien drehte, umgarnt Daisy (Jessica Harper) als Ersatz für seine verlorene Liebe zu Dorrie. / Le célèbre cinéaste Sandy Bates (Allen) fait la cour à Daisy (Jessica Harper) dans l'espoir de faire renaître son amour pour Dorrie.

STILL FROM 'STARDUST MEMORIES' (1980)
Sandy is beleaguered by fans at a film festival. / Fans
umlagern Sandy bei einem Filmfestival. / Sandy assailli
par ses admirateurs lors d'un festival de cinéma.

*"You want to do mankind a real service? Tell
funnier jokes."*
An alien to Sandy Bates (Woody Allen), *Stardust
Memories*

*„Du möchtest der Menschheit einen echten
Gefallen tun? Erzähl komischere Witze!"*
Ein Außerirdischer zu Sandy Bates (Woody Allen),
Stardust Memories

*« Vous voulez vraiment rendre service à
l'humanité ? Racontez des blagues plus drôles. »*
Un extraterrestre à Sandy Bates (Woody Allen), *Stardust
Memories*

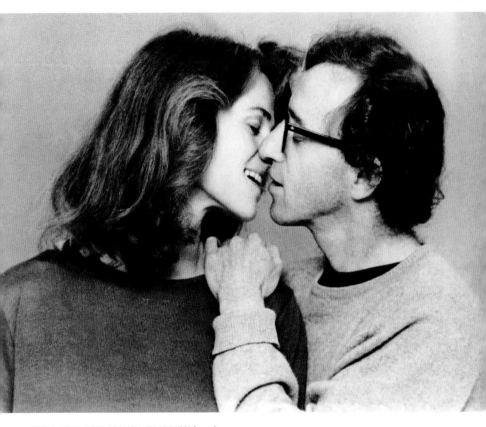

STILL FROM 'STARDUST MEMORIES' (1980)
Sandy is haunted by his past relationship with Dorrie (Charlotte Rampling), who had warned him that she was "fascinating but trouble." / Sandy kann seine Beziehung mit Dorrie (Charlotte Rampling) nicht vergessen, die ihn gewarnt hatte: Sie sei zwar „bezaubernd, aber schwierig". / Sandy est hanté par ses anciennes amours avec Dorrie (Charlotte Rampling), qui l'avait prévenu qu'elle était « fascinante mais dangereuse ».

PAGES 78/79
STILL FROM 'A MIDSUMMER NIGHT'S SEX COMEDY' (1982)
Stockbroker and crackpot inventor Andrew (Woody Allen) is attracted to intellectual Ariel (Mia Farrow), with whom he almost had an affair years earlier. / Der Börsenmakler und durchgeknallte Erfinder Andrew (Woody Allen) fühlt sich zu der intellektuellen Ariel (Mia Farrow) hingezogen, mit der er vor Jahren beinahe einmal eine Affäre gehabt hätte. / Agent de change et inventeur fou, Andrew (Woody Allen) est attiré par Ariel (Mia Farrow), une intello dont il a été amoureux dans sa jeunesse.

STILL FROM 'A MIDSUMMER NIGHT'S SEX COMEDY' (1982)
A group of friends spend a weekend in the country in turn-of-the-century upstate New York, and their ideas about love, lust, and reality are overturned. / Um die vorletzte Jahrhundertwende verbringt eine Gruppe von Freunden ein Wochenende auf dem Lande im Norden des Staates New York. Dabei werden ihre Vorstellungen von Liebe, Lust und Realität gründlich umgekrempelt. / Lors d'un week-end dans la campagne new-yorkaise au début du XXe siècle, trois couples d'amis confrontent leurs visions de l'amour, du désir et de la réalité.

"My grammar is terrible. Just terrible. There's a mass of corrections from The New Yorker all the time ... Saul Bellow, when I gave him his lines to say in Zelig, said, 'It's all right if I change this, isn't it? Because this is grammatically incorrect.'"
Woody Allen in 1988

„Meine Grammatik ist furchtbar. Einfach entsetzlich. Es gibt immer jede Menge Verbesserungen vom New Yorker ... Als ich Saul Bellow seinen Text für Zelig gab, sagte er: ‚Es ist doch in Ordnung, wenn ich das ändere, oder? Denn es ist grammatikalisch falsch.'"
Woody Allen 1988

STILL FROM 'A MIDSUMMER NIGHT'S SEX COMEDY' (1982)
Andrew and his wife, Adrian (Mary Steenburgen), rekindle their marriage on the kitchen stove. / Andrew und seine Frau Adrian (Mary Steenburgen) bei der Wiederbelebung ihrer Ehe auf dem Küchenherd. / Andrew et sa femme Adrian (Mary Steenburgen) ravivent la flamme de leur mariage sur le fourneau de la cuisine.

« Je suis nul en grammaire. Absolument nul. The New Yorker fait toujours des masses de corrections. [...] Quand je lui ai donné les répliques qu'il devait dire dans Zelig, Saul Bellow m'a demandé : "Cela ne t'ennuie pas que je change cette phrase ? Car elle est grammaticalement incorrecte." »
Woody Allen en 1988

STILL FROM 'ZELIG' (1983)
The human chameleon Leonard Zelig (Woody Allen)
between U. S. presidents Calvin Coolidge and Herbert
Hoover. / Das menschliche Chamäleon Leonard Zelig
(Woody Allen) zwischen den US-Präsidenten Calvin
Coolidge und Herbert Hoover. / Leonard Zelig (Woody
Allen), l'homme-caméléon, entre les présidents
américains Calvin Coolidge et Herbert Hoover.

STILL FROM 'ZELIG' (1983)
Unwilling to stand out from the crowd, Zelig will do
anything to assimilate. Here he is with champion boxer
Jack Dempsey. / Zelig tut alles, um nicht aufzufallen und
sich anzupassen. Hier ist er mit Boxchampion Jack
Dempsey zu sehen. / Incapable de sortir du lot, Zelig est
prêt à tout pour se fondre dans la masse, comme ici
avec le champion de boxe Jack Dempsey.

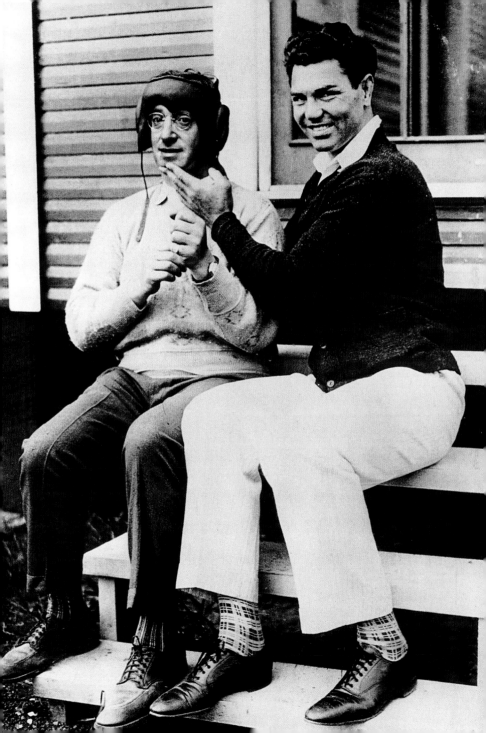

STILL FROM 'ZELIG' (1983)
A ticker-tape parade for Zelig and his analyst, Eudora Fletcher (Mia Farrow). / Eine Konfettiparade für Zelig und seine Psychoanalytikerin Eudora Fletcher (Mia Farrow). / Défilé sous une pluie de serpentins pour Zelig et sa psychanalyste, Eudora Fletcher (Mia Farrow).

STILL FROM 'ZELIG' (1983)
Allen's mock-documentary—Gordon Willis even used cameras from the period to shoot the film—explores the seeds of fascism and the cult of celebrity. / Allens Pseudodokumentarfilm, bei dem Gordon Willis sogar zeitgenössische Kameras einsetzte, beschäftigt sich mit den Wurzeln des Faschismus und dem Promikult. / Ce pseudo-documentaire – où Gordon Willis va jusqu'à utiliser des caméras d'époque pour le tournage – explore les germes du fascisme et le culte de la célébrité.

**STILL FROM 'BROADWAY DANNY ROSE'
(1984)**
Danny Rose (Woody Allen) is an old-time, nurturing
talent agent, here eluding mobsters who think he is in
love with Tina Vitale (Mia Farrow). / Danny Rose
(Woody Allen), ein Künstleragent der alten Schule, der
seine Klienten noch umsorgt, muss vor Mafiagangstern
fliehen, die glauben, er habe ein Verhältnis mit Tina
Vitale (Mia Farrow). / Danny Rose (Woody Allen), un
imprésario vieux jeu, tente d'échapper à des truands
convaincus qu'il est amoureux de Tina Vitale (Mia
Farrow).

*"I never plan anything. I don't rehearse anybody,
I don't post-sync anybody. I don't do a lot of
coverage ... People think this is part of my style,
but actually it's the lazy man's style."*
Woody Allen in 2005

*„Ich plane nie irgendetwas. Ich probe mit
niemandem, und ich synchronisiere niemanden
nach. Ich drehe nicht viel Überschuss ... Die Leute
denken, das gehöre zu meinem Stil, aber in
Wirklichkeit ist es reine Faulheit."*
Woody Allen 2005

*« Je ne planifie jamais rien. Je ne fais pas de
répétitions ni de post-synchro. Je ne multiplie pas
les prises. [...] Les gens croient que cela fait partie
de mon style, mais en réalité, c'est le style de la
paresse. »*
Woody Allen en 2005

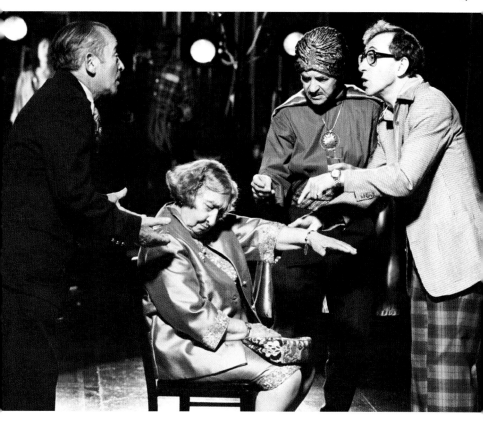

STILL FROM 'BROADWAY DANNY ROSE' (1984)

Danny Rose has complete faith in his acts, most of whom have little talent. This magician can hypnotize people but cannot snap them out of it. / Danny Rose hat größtes Vertrauen in die Fähigkeiten seiner Klienten, von denen die meisten jedoch recht talentfrei sind. Dieser Zauberkünstler kann Menschen zwar hypnotisieren, sie aber anschließend nicht wieder aufwecken. / Danny Rose a une foi aveugle en ses artistes, dont la plupart sont dénués de talent, comme ce magicien incapable de réveiller les cobayes qu'il a hypnotisés.

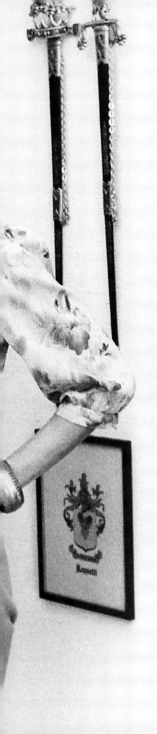

"I'm a lazy filmmaker. I don't like to go to grubby places or dangerous places. I don't like to work in excessive heat or excessive cold."
Woody Allen in 2005

„Ich bin ein fauler Filmemacher. Ich geh nicht gerne an schmuddelige oder gefährliche Orte. Ich mag nicht in übermäßiger Hitze oder Kälte arbeiten."
Woody Allen 2005

« Je suis un cinéaste paresseux. Je n'aime pas me rendre dans des endroits sordides ou des lieux dangereux. Je n'aime pas travailler par grand froid ou par une chaleur torride. »
Woody Allen en 2005

STILL FROM 'BROADWAY DANNY ROSE' (1984)
Brassy mob moll Tina looks and sounds intimidating, but she lacks confidence and direction, which Danny gives her during their adventure together. / Die ordinäre Gangsterbraut Tina sieht zwar Furcht einflößend aus und klingt auch so, aber in Wirklichkeit mangelt es ihr an Selbstvertrauen und Orientierung. Beides vermittelt ihr Danny während ihres gemeinsamen Abenteuers. / Malgré son allure intimidante et ses liens avec la mafia, Tina souffre d'un manque de confiance en elle auquel Danny remédiera au cours de leurs aventures.

**STILL FROM 'THE PURPLE ROSE OF CAIRO'
(1985)**
Cecilia (Mia Farrow) has a miserable marriage with
Monk (Danny Aiello), so she escapes to the movies in
Depression-era New Jersey. / In New Jersey während
der Weltwirtschaftskrise ist Cecilia (Mia Farrow)
unglücklich mit Monk (Danny Aiello) verheiratet und
entflieht in die Traumwelt des Kinos. / Durant la crise de
1929 dans le New Jersey, Cecilia (Mia Farrow), mal
mariée à Monk (Danny Aiello), fuit le quotidien dans les
salles obscures.

*"I just met a wonderful new man. He's fictional but
you can't have everything."*
Cecilia in *The Purple Rose of Cairo*

*„Ich habe gerade einen wunderbaren neuen Mann
kennengelernt. Er ist zwar nur erfunden, aber man
kann ja nicht alles haben."*
Cecilia in *The Purple Rose of Cairo*

*« Je viens de rencontrer un homme merveilleux.
Il est fictif, mais on ne peut pas tout avoir. »*
Cecilia dans *La Rose pourpre du Caire*

**STILL FROM 'THE PURPLE ROSE OF CAIRO'
(1985)**
Cecilia escapes ever further—into the film on the
screen, where she enjoys a nightclub spree in movie
Manhattan. / Cecilia flieht immer weiter - in den Film
hinein, der auf der Leinwand läuft. Hier genießt sie eine
Tour durch die Nachtclubs von Manhattan. / Fuyant le
réel, Cecilia pénètre dans le film projeté à l'écran pour
aller faire la fête dans un Manhattan en noir et blanc.

STILL FROM 'THE PURPLE ROSE OF CAIRO'
(1985)
Cecilia must decide between fantasy and reality. Will
she choose a future with the perfect but fictitious
hero of the movies Tom Baxter (Jeff Daniels)? / Cecilia
muss sich zwischen Fantasie und Wirklichkeit
entscheiden. Wird sie sich für eine Zukunft mit Tom
Baxter (Jeff Daniels) entscheiden, dem vollkommenen,
aber fiktiven Filmhelden? / Contrainte de choisir entre
l'imaginaire et la réalité, Cecilia choisira-t-elle Tom
Baxter (Jeff Daniels), héros de cinéma parfait mais
fictif ?

"The whole reason for Purple Rose was the ending.
It would have been a trivial movie with the other
[i. e., happy] ending."
Woody Allen in 1987

„Der ganze Grund für Purple Rose war der Schluss.
Mit dem anderen [d. h. dem glücklichen] Schluss
wäre es ein trivialer Film gewesen."
Woody Allen 1987

« La raison d'être de La Rose pourpre réside dans
le dénouement. Ce film aurait été banal avec
l'autre fin [le "happy end"]. »
Woody Allen en 1987

**STILL FROM 'THE PURPLE ROSE OF CAIRO'
(1985)**
Or will she choose the actor who plays Tom, Gil
Shepherd (Jeff Daniels)? It is one of Woody's most
intriguing films. / Oder wird sie Gil Shepherd (Jeff
Daniels) den Vorzug geben, dem Darsteller, der Tom
spielt? Dies ist einer von Woody Allens faszinierendsten
Filmen. / Ou choisira-t-elle Gil Shepherd (Jeff Daniels),
l'acteur qui joue le personnage ? Telle est l'interrogation
de Woody Allen dans l'un de ses films les plus
fascinants.

PAGES 94/95
**STILL FROM 'HANNAH AND HER SISTERS'
(1986)**
Mickey (Woody Allen), Hannah's ex-husband, is a
hypochondriac who discovers that he really is terribly
ill. / Mickey (Woody Allen), Hannahs früherer Ehemann,
ist ein Hypochonder, der herausfindet, dass er
tatsächlich an einer schrecklichen Krankheit leidet. /
Hypochondriaque de nature, Mickey (Woody Allen),
l'ex-mari de Hannah, découvre qu'il est réellement
atteint d'une terrible maladie.

**STILL FROM 'HANNAH AND HER SISTERS'
(1986)**
Elliot (Michael Caine), Hannah's present husband, is
attracted to one of Hannah's sisters, Lee (Barbara
Hershey). / Elliot (Michael Caine), Hannahs derzeitiger
Ehemann, fühlt sich zu ihrer Schwester Lee (Barbara
Hershey) hingezogen. / Elliot (Michael Caine), le mari
actuel de Hannah, est attiré par Lee (Barbara Hershey),
l'une des sœurs de sa femme.

*"A lot of my work is done in the reworking and
rewriting and reediting, like in Hannah [and Her
Sisters], where the entire second Thanksgiving
party was something that I did after the initial
filming."*
Woody Allen in 1987

*„Ein Großteil meiner Arbeit besteht aus der
nachträglichen Bearbeitung, dem Umschreiben
und dem Umschneiden, wie bei Hannah [und
ihre Schwestern], wo ich die gesamte zweite
Erntedankfeier nach den ursprünglichen
Dreharbeiten filmte."*
Woody Allen 1987

*« Je passe beaucoup de temps à remanier, réécrire
et remonter mes films, comme Hannah [et ses
sœurs], où la deuxième fête de Thanksgiving a été
entièrement ajoutée après le tournage initial. »*
Woody Allen en 1987

**STILL FROM 'HANNAH AND HER SISTERS'
(1986)**
The three sisters: perfect Hannah (Mia Farrow) makes
Lee feel inferior and unwittingly undermines Holly's
(Dianne Wiest) confidence. / Die drei Schwestern:
Die perfekte Hannah (Mia Farrow) macht Lee
Minderwertigkeitsgefühle und untergräbt unbewusst
auch Hollys (Dianne Wiest) Selbstvertrauen. / Les trois
sœurs : apparemment parfaite, Hannah (Mia Farrow)
donne des complexes à Lee et sape involontairement la
confiance de Holly (Dianne Wiest).

ON THE SET OF 'RADIO DAYS' (1987)
Woody directs Mia Farrow as Sally White, the Brooklyn cigarette girl who takes diction lessons and becomes a radio reporter of celebrity gossip. / Woody Allen gibt Mia Farrow Regieanweisungen. Sie spielt Sally White, eine Zigarettenverkäuferin aus Brooklyn, die Sprechunterricht nimmt und Klatschreporterin beim Rundfunk wird. / Woody dirige Mia Farrow dans le rôle de Sally White, la marchande de cigarettes de Brooklyn qui prend des cours de diction et devient chroniqueuse « people » à la radio.

PORTRAIT FOR 'RADIO DAYS' (1987)
This loose collection of anecdotes and memories is narrated by Woody Allen, represented as a boy by Seth Green. / Bei dieser lockeren Ansammlung von Anekdoten und Memoiren fungiert Woody Allen als Erzähler, während sein jüngeres Ich im Film von Seth Green dargestellt wird. / Dans ce recueil d'anecdotes et de souvenirs disparates, le narrateur (Woody Allen) apparaît sous les traits d'un jeune garçon (Seth Green).

STILL FROM 'SEPTEMBER' (1987)
The friendship of Stephanie (Dianne Wiest) and Lane (Mia Farrow) is tested in this somber, tragic ensemble film where, as one of the cast says, "The future is missing." / Die Freundschaft zwischen Stephanie (Dianne Wiest) und Lane (Mia Farrow) wird in diesem düsteren, tragischen Ensemblefilm auf die Probe gestellt, in dem, wie eine der Figuren sagt, „die Zukunft fehlt". / L'amitié de Stephanie (Dianne Wiest) et de Lane (Mia Farrow) est mise à l'épreuve dans ce film choral sombre et tragique où, comme le dit l'un des personnages, « l'avenir est absent ».

"September *is a picture that I think that I shot better than any before. I did it with more sophistication because we were all in that house and the camera was moving constantly and there were tons of things happening off-camera, which is a way I would never have shot my early films.*"
Woody Allen in 1987

„September *ist ein Film, den ich, glaube ich, besser drehte als irgendeinen meiner früheren Filme. Ich tat es mit mehr Raffinesse, weil wir alle in diesem Haus waren und sich die Kamera ständig bewegte, und es passierten Unmengen von Dingen außerhalb des Bildes, was ich in meinen früheren Filmen niemals gemacht hätte.*"
Woody Allen 1987

ON THE SET OF 'SEPTEMBER' (1987)
Jack Warden, Elaine Stritch, and Mia Farrow listen to
Woody Allen. This was the second version of the film.
Allen did not like the first version, so he refilmed it with
a different cast. / Jack Warden, Elaine Stritch und Mia
Farrow hören Woody Allen zu. Dies war die zweite
Fassung des Films. Allen mochte die erste Version nicht
und drehte den Film mit anderer Besetzung noch
einmal neu. / Jack Warden, Elaine Stritch et Mia Farrow
écoutent Woody Allen qui, n'aimant pas la première
version du film, en tourne une seconde avec une
distribution différente.

« Je pense que September est mieux réalisé que
tous les films précédents. La réalisation est plus
recherchée, car nous étions tous dans la même
maison, la caméra bougeait en permanence et il se
passait énormément de choses hors champ, ce qui
ne se serait jamais produit auparavant. »
Woody Allen en 1987

STILL FROM 'ANOTHER WOMAN' (1988)
Another drama: Sandy Dennis and Ian Holm play the
friend and second husband of Marion, who takes stock
of her life when she turns 50. / Noch ein Drama: Sandy
Dennis und Ian Holm spielen die Freundin und den
zweiten Ehemann von Marion, die Bilanz ihres Lebens
zieht, als sie 50 wird. / Autre drame : Sandy Dennis et
Ian Holm incarnent l'amie et le second époux de
Marion, qui fait le point sur sa vie au passage de la
cinquantaine.

"I put all I felt about turning 50 into Marion [in
Another Woman]. It took me at least a year to get
over it."
Woody Allen in 1987

„Ich packte all meine Gefühle über meinen 50.
Geburtstag in Marion [in Eine andere Frau] hinein.
Ich brauchte mindestens ein Jahr, um damit fertig
zu werden."
Woody Allen 1987

« Tout ce que j'éprouvais au passage de la
cinquantaine, je l'ai mis dans le personnage de
Marion [dans Une autre femme]. Il m'a fallu au
moins un an pour m'en remettre. »
Woody Allen en 1987

STILL FROM 'ANOTHER WOMAN' (1988)
Marion (Gena Rowlands) goes for a walk with Larry
Lewis (Gene Hackman), a writer who loved her and who
based a character in a novel on her. / Marion (Gena
Rowlands) geht mit Larry Lewis (Gene Hackman)
spazieren, einem Schriftsteller, der sie einmal liebte
und sie zur Vorlage für eine Figur in einem seiner
Romane machte. / Marion (Gena Rowlands) se promène
avec Larry Lewis (Gene Hackman), un écrivain
autrefois amoureux d'elle qui s'en est inspiré pour un
personnage de roman.

PAGES 104/105
STILL FROM 'NEW YORK STORIES' (1989)
"I guess I am a creature of the pavement, of Madison
Square Garden, of the restaurants, of the bookstores—
you know, the streets."—Woody Allen (2005) / „Ich
denke, ich bin ein Geschöpf der Gehsteige, des Madison
Square Garden, der Restaurants, der Buchläden - Sie
wissen schon: der Straße." — Woody Allen (2005) /
« Mon élément, c'est le bitume, Madison Square
Garden, les restaurants, les librairies... bref, la rue. »
— Woody Allen (2005)

**STILL FROM 'CRIMES AND MISDEMEANORS'
(1989)**
The film's tragic story concerns Judah (Martin Landau),
who wants to dispose of his threatening mistress
(Anjelica Huston). / Die tragische Geschichte von Judah
(Martin Landau), der seine Geliebte (Anjelica Huston)
loswerden möchte, die ihn bedroht. / L'histoire tragique
de Judah (Martin Landau), qui tente de se débarrasser
de son encombrante maîtresse (Anjelica Huston).

"*Someone else doing* Crimes and Misdemeanors
*could have a brilliant murder scene. Alfred
Hitchcock or Martin Scorsese—a guy knocks on the
door holding flowers and she answers it and what
ensues is a minute and a half of brilliant cinema.
The only explanation I can give is that for me,
because I'm more writer than anything, all that
stuff becomes material for me to make my points
on, to talk about, to philosophize over.*"
Woody Allen in 2006

„*Wenn jemand anders Verbrechen und andere
Kleinigkeiten gemacht hätte, dann hätte er eine
geniale Mordszene drehen können. Alfred
Hitchcock oder Martin Scorsese - ein Typ klopft
an die Tür, mit einem Strauß Blumen in der Hand,
sie öffnet, und dann folgen anderthalb Minuten
geniales Kino. Die einzige Erklärung, die ich für
mich abgeben kann, ist: Weil ich zuallererst
Schriftsteller bin, wird all dies für mich zum
Material, mit dem ich meine Aussage mache -
über das geredet und philosophiert wird.*"
Woody Allen 2006

**STILL FROM 'CRIMES AND MISDEMEANORS'
(1989)**
The film's tragicomic story concerns Cliff (Woody Allen),
who is married but attracted to another woman, Halley
(Mia Farrow). / Der Film erzählt die tragikomische
Geschichte von Cliff (Woody Allen), der zwar
verheiratet ist, sich aber zu einer anderen Frau – Halley
(Mia Farrow) – hingezogen fühlt. / La seconde histoire,
tragi-comique, concerne Cliff (Woody Allen), un homme
marié attiré par une autre femme (Mia Farrow).

« Si Crimes et délits avait été tourné par quelqu'un
d'autre, il aurait pu y avoir une formidable scène
de meurtre. Chez Alfred Hitchcock ou Martin
Scorsese, un type frappe à la porte avec un
bouquet à la main, elle ouvre et il s'ensuit une
minute et demie de cinéma d'anthologie. La seule
explication que je peux donner, c'est que pour moi,
du fait que je suis plus un écrivain qu'autre chose,
tout cela devient matière à discuter, à démontrer,
à philosopher. »
Woody Allen en 2006

**STILL FROM 'CRIMES AND MISDEMEANORS'
(1989)**
Judah enlists the help of his criminal brother (Jerry
Orbach) to murder his mistress. / Judah engagiert
seinen kriminellen Bruder (Jerry Orbach) als Killer, um
sich seiner Geliebten zu entledigen. / C'est à son frère
(Jerry Orbach), qui a mal tourné, que Judah fait appel
pour assassiner sa maîtresse.

"Woody's life is his work. He is just not a relaxer."
Diane Keaton

„Woodys Leben ist seine Arbeit. Er ist einfach nicht
der Typ, der sich entspannt."
Diane Keaton

« Woody vit pour son travail. Il n'est pas du genre à
se détendre. »
Diane Keaton

**STILL FROM 'CRIMES AND MISDEMEANORS'
(1989)**
At the end of one of Woody's best films, Judah and Cliff
assess the gains and losses from their moral crimes and
misdemeanors. / Am Schluss eines der besten Woody-
Allen-Filme ziehen Judah und Cliff Bilanz über die
Gewinne und Verluste aus ihren moralischen
Verbrechen (crimes) und Vergehen (misdemeanors). /
À la fin du film – l'un des meilleurs de Woody Allen –,
Judah et Cliff dressent le bilan de leurs divers crimes
et délits.

STILL FROM 'ALICE' (1990)
Like 'The Purple Rose of Cairo,' this film has a touch
of fantasy, as Alice (Mia Farrow) is attracted to a
handsome stranger (Joe Mantegna). / Genau wie *The
Purple Rose of Cairo*, so hat auch dieser Film, in dem
sich Alice (Mia Farrow) zu einem gut aussehenden
Fremden (Joe Mantegna) hingezogen fühlt, einen Hauch
von Fantastik. / Comme *La Rose pourpre du Caire*, ce
film vire au fantastique lorsque Alice (Mia Farrow) se
sent attirée par un bel étranger (Joe Mantegna).

"Richard Schickel ... wrote a very nice essay about
me once, saying that my audience left me at a
certain point. And I thought that was the one thing
he had wrong. It was that I left them: they didn't
leave me."
Woody Allen in 2000

„Richard Schickel ... schrieb einmal einen sehr
netten Essay über mich, in dem er sagte, das
Publikum habe mich an einem bestimmten Punkt
verlassen. Und ich dachte: Das war die einzige
Sache, die er falsch verstanden hatte. Es war
nämlich so, dass ich es verlassen hatte - es hatte
nicht mich verlassen."
Woody Allen 2000

STILL FROM 'ALICE' (1990)
Through the power of some potent herbs, Alice becomes invisible and observes the infidelities of her husband (William Hurt). / Ein paar starke Kräuter machen Alice unsichtbar, und so wird sie Zeugin der Untreue ihres Ehemanns (William Hurt). / Grâce au puissant élixir d'un médecin chinois, Alice devient invisible et observe les infidélités de son mari (William Hurt).

«Richard Schickel [...] a écrit un très bel essai à mon sujet, où il explique qu'à un moment donné, le public s'est détaché de moi. C'est le seul point sur lequel je pense qu'il se trompe. Ce n'est pas le public qui s'est détaché de moi, c'est moi qui me suis détaché de lui.»
Woody Allen en 2000

STILL FROM 'SCENES FROM A MALL' (1991)
In this comedy directed by Paul Mazursky, Nick
(Woody Allen) and Deborah Fifer (Bette Midler) are a
Los Angeles couple who reveal their infidelities on their
16th wedding anniversary. / In dieser Komödie, bei der
Paul Mazursky Regie führte, decken Nick (Woody Allen)
und Deborah Fifer (Bette Midler), ein Ehepaar aus
Los Angeles, ausgerechnet an ihrem 16. Hochzeitstag
ihre Seitensprünge auf. / Dans cette comédie réalisée
par Paul Mazursky, Nick (Woody Allen) et Deborah Fifer
(Bette Midler) s'avouent leurs infidélités au cours de
leur 16ᵉ anniversaire de mariage.

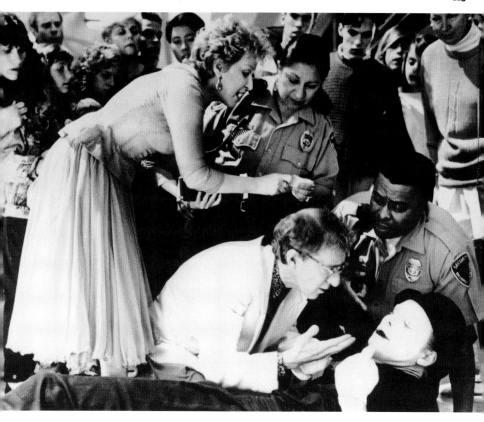

STILL FROM 'SCENES FROM A MALL' (1991)
Reportedly, Woody Allen had never been inside a mall
before this film was shot. Bill Irwin plays the mime. /
Angeblich war Woody Allen noch nie in einem
Einkaufszentrum, bevor er diesen Film drehte. Den
Pantomimen spielt hier Bill Irwin. / Woody Allen, qui
prétend n'avoir jamais mis les pieds dans un centre
commercial avant le tournage, est ici avec Bill Irwin dans
le rôle du mime.

STILL FROM 'SHADOWS AND FOG' (1992)
The killer is at large in this homage to German
Expressionist films, beautifully photographed by Carlo
Di Palma. / Carlo Di Palma leistete ausgezeichnete
Kameraarbeit in dieser Hommage an die großen
Expressionisten des deutschen Films, in der es um
einen Mörder geht, der die Gegend unsicher macht. /
Un tueur rôde dans cet hommage au cinéma
expressionniste allemand, magnifiquement
photographié par Carlo Di Palma.

"There are certain directors, such as Sidney Lumet,
who have affectionate relationships with actors,
but I've never been able to work that way. I give as
much contact as is required professionally ... I know
there's not a buoyant atmosphere on my set."
Woody Allen

„Es gibt bestimmte Regisseure, wie etwa Sidney
Lumet, die sehr herzlich mit Schauspielern
umgehen, aber so konnte ich noch nie arbeiten.
Ich pflege so viel Kontakt, wie es die Arbeit
erfordert ... Ich weiß selbst, dass es bei meinen
Dreharbeiten nicht heiter und ausgelassen zugeht."
Woody Allen

ON THE SET OF 'SHADOWS AND FOG' (1992)
Woody has always had the ability to attact big names
for small projects. This film features John Malkovich,
Madonna (both pictured), and Jodie Foster, among
others. / Woody Allen besaß stets die Fähigkeit, große
Namen für kleine Projekte zu gewinnen. In diesem Film
treten unter anderem John Malkovich, Madonna (beide
im Bild) und Jodie Foster auf. / Woody Allen a toujours
eu le don d'attirer de grands noms pour de petits
projets. Ce film met notamment en scène John
Malkovich, Madonna (tous deux sur la photo) et
Jodie Foster.

« *Certains metteurs en scène, comme Sidney
Lumet, ont des relations affectueuses avec les
acteurs, mais je n'ai jamais pu travailler de cette
façon. Avec moi, les contacts se limitent à ce qui
est nécessaire professionnellement. [...] Il ne règne
pas une atmosphère enjouée sur mes tournages.* »
Woody Allen

STILL FROM 'HUSBANDS AND WIVES' (1992)
Jack (Sydney Pollack) breaks up with his wife and three
weeks later takes up with Sam (Lysette Anthony) in
this intense study of relationships. / In dieser starken
Beziehungsstudie trennt sich Jack (Sydney Pollack) von
seiner Frau und lässt sich schon drei Wochen später mit
Sam (Lysette Anthony) ein. / Une étude incisive sur les
relations sentimentales où Jack (Sydney Pollack), à
peine séparé de sa femme, se remet trois semaines plus
tard avec Sam (Lysette Anthony).

"Husbands and Wives was just a fun experiment.
That was a picture that I wanted to be ugly.
I didn't want anything to match on it or be refined
or cut well. I wanted it to be an unattractive
picture to see."
Woody Allen in 2005

„Ehemänner und Ehefrauen war einfach nur ein
witziges Experiment. Das war ein Film, von dem
ich wollte, dass er hässlich wird. Ich wollte nicht,
dass irgendetwas passte oder elegant oder gut
geschnitten war. Ich wollte, dass es für den
Zuschauer ein unattraktiver Film ist."
Woody Allen 2005

STILL FROM 'HUSBANDS AND WIVES' (1992)
Judy (Mia Farrow) hides her true feelings from
everybody, including herself. / Judy (Mia Farrow)
verbirgt ihre wahren Gefühle – auch vor sich selbst. /
Judy (Mia Farrow) cache ses véritables sentiments à
tout le monde, y compris à elle-même.

« Maris et femmes était une expérience amusante.
Je voulais que ce film soit laid. Je voulais que rien
ne soit assorti, raffiné ou bien coupé. Je voulais
que ce film ne soit pas beau à voir. »
Woody Allen en 2005

STILL FROM 'HUSBANDS AND WIVES' (1992)
Though she is married to Gabe, Judy begins to fall in
love with her editor Michael (Liam Neeson). / Obwohl
sie mit Gabe verheiratet ist, verliebt sich Judy
allmählich in ihren Redakteur Michael (Liam Neeson). /
Bien que mariée à Gabe, Judy commence à s'éprendre
de son éditeur, Michael (Liam Neeson).

*"To me it's a damn shame that the universe doesn't
have any God or meaning, and yet only when you
can accept that can you then go on to lead what
these people call a Christian life—that is, a decent,
moral life."*
Woody Allen in 2006

*„Ich finde es verdammt schade, dass das
Universum keinen Gott oder keinen Sinn hat -
aber dennoch muss man diese Tatsache zunächst
hinnehmen, um dann das zu führen, was diese
Leute ein ‚christliches Leben' nennen - also ein
anständiges, moralisches Leben."*
Woody Allen 2006

STILL FROM 'HUSBANDS AND WIVES' (1992)
Gabe (Woody Allen) knows that a relationship with his
student Rain (Juliette Lewis) would be too emotionally
dangerous for him. He ends the film alone. / Gabe
(Woody Allen) weiß, dass eine Beziehung zu seiner
Schülerin Rain (Juliette Lewis) emotional zu gefährlich
für ihn wäre, und so ist er am Ende des Films allein. /
Conscient du péril émotionnel que représenterait une
liaison avec son étudiante, Rain (Juliette Lewis), Gabe
(Woody Allen) se retrouve seul à la fin du film.

*« Pour moi, c'est sacrément dommage que Dieu
n'existe pas et que l'univers n'ait aucun sens ;
pourtant, il faut l'admettre pour pouvoir mener
ce que certains appellent une vie chrétienne,
c'est-à-dire une existence honnête et morale. »*
Woody Allen en 2006

PAGES 120/121
**STILL FROM 'MANHATTAN MURDER
MYSTERY' (1993)**
Woody reteams with Diane Keaton as a husband and
wife caught in a murder mystery. / Woody Allen und
Diane Keaton stehen wieder gemeinsam vor der
Kamera: als Ehepaar, das in eine geheimnisvolle
Mordgeschichte verwickelt wird. / Woody refait équipe
avec Diane Keaton dans le rôle d'un couple marié
confronté à une affaire de meurtre.

STILL FROM 'MANHATTAN MURDER MYSTERY' (1993)
Carol Lipton (Diane Keaton) believes that her neighbor
Paul (Jerry Adler) has killed his wife, and drags her
husband, Larry (Woody Allen), along. / Carol Lipton
(Diane Keaton) glaubt, dass ihr Nachbar Paul (Jerry
Adler) seine Frau ermordet hat, und sie schleppt ihren
Ehemann Larry (Woody Allen) mit. / Convaincue que
son voisin Paul (Jerry Adler) a tué sa femme, Carol
Lipton (Diane Keaton) entraîne son mari Larry (Woody
Allen) dans l'aventure.

*"I just had a good time making that movie
[Manhattan Murder Mystery]. And it came out
very well. It's really one of my best movies."*
Woody Allen in 2006

*„Ich hatte einfach nur einen Riesenspaß bei den
Dreharbeiten zu diesem Film [Manhattan Murder
Mystery]. Und er ist auch sehr gelungen. Es ist
wirklich einer meiner besten Filme."*
Woody Allen 2006

STILL FROM 'MANHATTAN MURDER MYSTERY' (1993)
The Liptons gather their friends to catch the killer. The taped voice of the killer's girlfriend will lure him into their trap. / Die Liptons trommeln ihre Freunde zusammen, um den Mörder zu fassen. Die Stimme seiner Freundin auf einem Tonband soll ihn in die Falle locken. / Les Lipton rassemblent leurs amis pour confondre le coupable, qu'ils comptent attirer dans leurs filets grâce à un enregistrement de la voix de sa petite amie.

« Je me suis bien amusé en faisant ce film [Meurtre mystérieux à Manhattan]. *Et je suis très satisfait du résultat. C'est vraiment un de mes meilleurs films. »*
Woody Allen en 2006

**STILL FROM 'BULLETS OVER BROADWAY'
(1994)**
Playwright David Shayne (John Cusack) says that he
is an uncompromising artist, yet he changes his play
because he is enamored of his leading lady, Helen
Sinclair (Dianne Wiest). / Der Dramatiker David Shayne
(John Cusack) sieht sich als kompromissloser Künstler,
und doch schreibt er sein Stück um, weil er in seine
Hauptdarstellerin Helen Sinclair (Dianne Wiest) verliebt
ist. / Bien qu'il prétende être un artiste sans concession,
le dramaturge David Shayne (John Cusack) modifie sa
pièce par amour pour l'actrice principale, Helen Sinclair
(Dianne Wiest).

*"[John] Cusack is one of those guys like Liam
Neeson and Michael Caine, incapable of a
graceless moment in front of the camera."*
Woody Allen in 2000

*„[John] Cusack ist einer dieser Kerle wie Liam
Neeson und Michael Caine, die einfach unfähig
sind, einen einzigen Augenblick vor der Kamera
reizlos zu wirken."*
Woody Allen 2000

*« [John] Cusack est de ces hommes, comme
Liam Neeson et Michael Caine, qui sont incapables
d'être un seul instant dénués de grâce devant
la caméra. »*
Woody Allen en 2000

STILL FROM 'BULLETS OVER BROADWAY'
(1994)
More compromises. David Shayne has to deal with
mobster Nick Valenti (Joe Viterelli, second left), bad
actor Olive Neal (Jennifer Tilly, right), and his own lack
of talent. / Noch mehr Kompromisse: David Shayne
muss sich mit dem Mafioso Nick Valenti (Joe Viterelli,
2. von links), der schlechten Schauspielerin Olive Neal
(Jennifer Tilly, rechts) und seiner eigenen Talentlosigkeit
herumplagen. / Autres concessions : David Shayne doit
composer avec le gangster Nick Valenti (Joe Viterelli,
deuxième à gauche), la mauvaise actrice Olive Neal
(Jennifer Tilly, à droite) et son propre manque de talent.

STILL FROM 'MIGHTY APHRODITE' (1995)
Lenny (Woody Allen) begins to wonder about the
mother of his adopted son, not knowing it is Linda. /
Lenny (Woody Allen) fragt sich, wer die Mutter seines
Adoptivsohns sein könnte, und ahnt nicht, dass es Linda
ist. / Lenny (Woody Allen) commence à s'interroger sur
la mère de son fils adoptif, sans savoir que c'est Linda.

STILL FROM 'MIGHTY APHRODITE' (1995)
Mira Sorvino, as prostitute Linda, won an Oscar for best
supporting actress. / Mira Sorvino erhielt für ihre Rolle
der Prostituierten Linda den „Oscar" als beste
Nebendarstellerin. / Mira Sorvino, qui incarne la
prostituée Linda, remporte l'oscar du Meilleur
second rôle.

**STILL FROM 'EVERYONE SAYS I LOVE YOU'
(1996)**
"Alan [Alda] is a perfect example of a guy who can
take material that has the potential to be funny but is
not funny in anyone's hands except an extremely
skilled performer, and he'll make it sing."—Woody Allen
(2005) / „Alan [Alda] ist das perfekte Beispiel für einen
Typen, der potenziell witziges Material nehmen kann,
das aber nur in den Händen eines äußerst talentierten
Darstellers komisch ist – und der bringt es zum
Singen." – Woody Allen (2005) / « Alan [Alda] est
l'exemple même du type capable de faire des merveilles
avec une scène potentiellement drôle, mais qui ne le
sera qu'entre les mains d'un acteur extrêmement
talentueux. » — Woody Allen (2005)

*"When I was making [Everyone Says I Love You],
the people in the music department were saying,
'They can't sing!' And the distributors were saying,
'They can't sing!' And I kept saying, 'Yes, I know,
that's the point. If they sing like they do in the
shower, like regular people, that's the idea.'"*
Woody Allen in 2000

**STILL FROM 'EVERYONE SAYS I LOVE YOU'
(1996)**
Skylar (Drew Barrymore) and Holden (Edward Norton)
are thinking, and singing, about marriage. / Skylar (Drew
Barrymore) und Holden (Edward Norton) denken nach
– und singen – über die Ehe. / Skylar (Drew Barrymore)
et Holden (Edward Norton) pensent au mariage... en
chantant.

„Als ich [Alle sagen: I Love You] drehte, sagten die
Leute in der Musikabteilung: ‚Die können nicht
singen!' Und der Verleih sagte: ‚Die können nicht
singen!' Und ich sagte immer wieder: ‚Ja, das weiß
ich. Darum geht es ja! Wenn sie so singen wie unter
der Dusche, wie normale Menschen, dann ist es
genau das, was ich will.'"
Woody Allen 2000

« Quand je tournais [Tout le monde dit "I Love
You"], les gens du département musical me
disaient : "Ils ne savent pas chanter !" Et les
distributeurs me répétaient : "Ils ne savent pas
chanter !" Et je leur répondais : "Je sais, c'est fait
exprès. S'ils chantent comme on chante sous
la douche, comme les gens normaux, c'est là
toute l'idée." »
Woody Allen en 2000

**STILL FROM 'DECONSTRUCTING HARRY'
(1997)**
Woody plays blocked novelist Harry Block, whose
ex-girlfriend (Elisabeth Shue) and friend Larry (Billy
Crystal) plan to marry. / Woody spielt den Romanautor
Harry Block, der unter einer Schreibblockade leidet
und dessen Exfreundin (Elisabeth Shue) seinen Freund
Larry (Billy Crystal) heiraten möchte. / Woody incarne
Harry Block, un écrivain en panne d'inspiration, dont
l'ami Larry (Billy Crystal) s'apprête à épouser l'ex-petite
amie (Elisabeth Shue).

"At their best, jokes are a vehicle to present a
character."
Woody Allen in 1974

„Witze sind bestenfalls ein Vehikel zur Darstellung
eines Charakters."
Woody Allen 1974

« Au mieux, les blagues sont un support pour
décrire un personnage. »
Woody Allen en 1974

**STILL FROM 'DECONSTRUCTING HARRY'
(1997)**
Another impressive cast: Demi Moore (pictured), Robin
Williams, Tobey Maguire, Judy Davis, and Mariel
Hemingway, among others. / Wieder eine
eindrucksvolle Besetzung: unter anderem Demi Moore
(im Bild), Robin Williams, Tobey Maguire, Judy Davis
und Mariel Hemingway. / Autre distribution
impressionnante : Demi Moore (en photo), Robin
Williams, Tobey Maguire, Judy Davis et Mariel
Hemingway, parmi d'autres.

STILL FROM 'WILD MAN BLUES' (1997)
Documentary filmmaker Barbara Kopple followed
Woody Allen on a musical tour of Europe. Here he
rides in a gondola with Soon-Yi Previn, whom he married
in 1997. / Die Dokumentarfilmerin Barbara Kopple folgte
Woody Allen auf seiner Jazz-Tournee durch Europa.
Hier fährt er in einer Gondel mit Soon-Yi Previn, die er
1997 heiratete. / Suivi par la documentariste Barbara
Kopple lors d'une tournée musicale en Europe, Woody
Allen se promène en gondole avec Soon-Yi Previn, qu'il
a épousée en 1997.

"I'm not social. I don't get an enormous input from
the rest of the world. I wish I could get out more
and mingle, because I could write better things.
But I can't."
Woody Allen in 1974

„Ich bin kein geselliger Mensch. Der Rest der Welt
gibt mir nicht sonderlich viel. Ich wünschte, ich
könnte mehr rausgehen und mich unter die Leute
mischen, weil ich dann bessere Sachen schreiben
könnte, aber ich kann es nicht."
Woody Allen 1974

« Je ne suis pas quelqu'un de sociable. Les autres
ne m'apportent pas grand-chose. J'aimerais sortir
et avoir une vie sociale, car ce serait bon pour mon
travail. Mais j'en suis incapable. »
Woody Allen en 1974

STILL FROM 'WILD MAN BLUES' (1997)
The film captures his lifelong love of the clarinet and
New Orleans jazz. / Der Film zeichnet seine lebenslange
Liebe zur Klarinette und zum New-Orleans-Jazz nach. /
Le film retrace sa passion de toujours pour la clarinette
et le jazz de La Nouvelle-Orléans.

PAGES 134/135
STILL FROM 'ANTZ' (1998)
Woody voiced the role of Z-4195, or Z (right), in this
animated film directed by Eric Darnell and Tim Johnson. /
In diesem Animationsfilm unter der Regie von Eric
Darnell und Tim Johnson lieh Woody Allen der Ameise
Z-4195, kurz „Z" genannt, in der Originalfassung seine
Stimme (rechts). / Dans ce film d'animation réalisé par
Eric Darnell et Tim Johnson, Woody prête sa voix à la
fourmi Z-4195, alias Z (à droite).

STILL FROM 'CELEBRITY' (1998)
This film, along with 'Zelig,' explores both the lure and the destructiveness of fame. Charlize Theron is on the catwalk. / Dieser Film beschäftigt sich, ebenso wie *Zelig*, mit den Verlockungen und Gefahren des Ruhms. Auf dem Laufsteg ist hier Charlize Theron zu sehen. / Tout comme *Zelig*, ce film se penche sur le pouvoir d'attraction et de destruction de la célébrité, illustrée par Charlize Theron dans ce défilé de mode.

STILL FROM 'CELEBRITY' (1998)
Lee (Kenneth Branagh) is a media journalist who prides himself on his integrity. Here he gambles with celebrity Brandon Darrow (Leonardo DiCaprio). / Lee (Kenneth Branagh) ist ein Journalist, der stolz auf seine Integrität ist. Hier ist er beim Glücksspiel mit dem Promi Brandon Darrow (Leonardo DiCaprio) zu sehen. / Lee (Kenneth Branagh), un journaliste fier de son intégrité, joue ici en compagnie d'une célébrité, Brandon Darrow (Leonardo DiCaprio).

STILL FROM 'SWEET AND LOWDOWN' (1999)
Writer Blanche Williams (Uma Thurman) is excited by
Emmet Ray (Sean Penn), a jazz guitarist whose artistic
brilliance coexists with a horrible personality. / Die
Schriftstellerin Blanche Williams (Uma Thurman) ist von
Emmet Ray (Sean Penn) fasziniert, einem künstlerisch
genialen Jazzgitarristen mit einem fürchterlichen
Charakter. / L'écrivain Blanche Williams (Uma Thurman)
est attirée par Emmet Ray (Sean Penn), un guitariste de
jazz dont le génie artistique se double d'un caractère
exécrable.

STILL FROM 'SWEET AND LOWDOWN' (1999)
The script was originally written by Woody in the late
1960s and called 'The Jazz Baby.' United Artists,
expecting a comedy, hesitated, and Allen substituted
the script for 'Bananas.' / Woody Allen hatte das
Drehbuch ursprünglich Ende der 1960er-Jahre
geschrieben und „The Jazz Baby" betitelt. United
Artists, die eine Komödie von ihm erwarteten,
zauderten, und Allen lieferte ihnen stattdessen
Bananas. / Écrit à la fin des années 1960 sous le titre
« The Jazz Baby », le scénario fut tièdement accueilli
par United Artists, qui attendait une comédie, et Woody
Allen lui substitua *Bananas*.

STILL FROM 'SWEET AND LOWDOWN' (1999)
Hattie (Samantha Morton), a mute, can only express her love for Emmet through her actions—here tearing his clothes off. / Die stumme Hattie (Samantha Morton) kann ihre Liebe zu Emmet nur durch ihr Handeln ausdrücken - indem sie ihm beispielsweise, wie hier, die Kleider vom Leib reißt. / Muette, Hattie (Samantha Morton) ne peut exprimer son amour pour Emmet que par des gestes, comme lui arracher ses vêtements.

"For me comedy just flows and I feel in control and I have that feeling that a musician feels who can play … With serious stuff, I'm more at sea and I flounder more and I don't trust myself."
Woody Allen in 2005

„Für mich fließt Komödie einfach so, und ich habe das Gefühl, dass ich die Kontrolle besitze, so wie sich ein Musiker fühlt, der etwas spielen kann … Bei ernsteren Stoffen gerate ich mehr ins Schwimmen und traue mir selbst nicht."
Woody Allen 2005

« Pour moi, la comédie coule de source, je me sens maître de ce que je fais, je me sens comme un musicien qui sait jouer de son instrument. [...] Avec des sujets plus sérieux, je me sens largué, je patauge et je n'ai pas confiance en moi. »
Woody Allen en 2005

STILL FROM 'SWEET AND LOWDOWN' (1999)
Lowdown Emmet expresses his love for Hattie through
his sweet music. This is the moment she falls in love with
him. / Der widerliche (*low-down*) Emmet drückt seine
Liebe zu Hattie durch seine süße (*sweet*) Musik aus.
Hier ist der Augenblick, in dem sie sich in ihn verliebt. /
L'exécrable Emmet ne peut exprimer son amour pour
Hattie qu'à travers sa douce musique, qui fait chavirer le
cœur de la jeune femme.

STILL FROM 'SMALL TIME CROOKS' (2000)
The crooks tunnel from the basement of a restaurant into a bank; however, they make their fortune on the cookies they sell in the restaurant. / Die Ganoven graben einen Tunnel vom Keller eines Restaurants in eine Bank, doch ihr Vermögen verdienen sie mit den Keksen, die sie im Restaurant verkaufen. / Après avoir creusé un tunnel entre la cave d'une pâtisserie et la banque voisine, les escrocs font fortune en vendant des cookies.

STILL FROM 'SMALL TIME CROOKS' (2000)
Amid bungled frauds and robberies, the film tells the story of Ray (Woody Allen) and Frenchy Winkler (Tracey Ullman), who break up and reconcile. / Zwischen verpatzten Betrügereien und Raubversuchen erzählt der Film die Geschichte von Ray (Woody Allen) und Frenchy Winkler (Tracey Ullman), die sich erst trennen und dann wieder versöhnen. / Cette histoire d'escroqueries et de cambriolages ratés est aussi celle de Ray (Woody Allen) et de Frenchy Winkler (Tracey Ullman), un couple qui se déchire et se réconcilie.

STILL FROM 'SMALL TIME CROOKS' (2000)
Ray tries to substitute a paste necklace for a valuable one in another ill-considered scheme. / Ein weiterer unausgegorener Plan sieht vor, dass Ray ein Strass-halsband gegen ein kostbares austauscht. / Dans son énième plan foireux, Ray tente de substituer un collier en strass à un bijou de valeur.

"Well, in the last couple of years—I've always done long takes—I've elaborated to really long takes ... I've taken to choreographing a lot of that in recent years because I enjoy it and it saves me from covering ... I like to go as long as the scene holds without a cut. If you can make it hold, great."
Woody Allen in 2005

„*Nun, ich habe immer schon lange Einstellungen gedreht, aber in den letzten paar Jahren habe ich wirklich lange Einstellungen ausgetüftelt ... In letzter Zeit habe ich mir angewöhnt, viel auf diese Art zu choreografieren, weil es mir Spaß macht und die zusätzlichen Einstellungen erspart ... Ich mag es, eine Szene so lange zu drehen, wie sie sich ohne Schnitt trägt. Wenn man das schafft - großartig.*"
Woody Allen 2005

STILL FROM 'SMALL TIME CROOKS' (2000)
Frenchy hires David (Hugh Grant) to teach them about the arts, so that they can enter high society, but all they find is a better class of crook. / Frenchy engagiert David (Hugh Grant), um ihnen Kunstverständnis zu vermitteln, damit sie Zugang zur „besseren Gesellschaft" erlangen, doch sie finden dort nur eine bessere Sorte von Ganoven vor. / Soucieuse de s'initier à l'art pour pénétrer dans la haute société, Frenchy emploie les services de David (Hugh Grant) et ne découvre qu'une race supérieure d'escrocs.

« J'ai toujours fait de longs plans séquences, mais depuis un ou deux ans, je me suis mis à faire des plans vraiment longs. [...] Ces dernières années, je me suis mis à beaucoup chorégraphier les plans séquences, ça me plaît et ça m'évite de multiplier les prises. [...] J'aime filmer toute la scène d'un seul trait. Si ça tient la route, tant mieux. »
Woody Allen en 2005

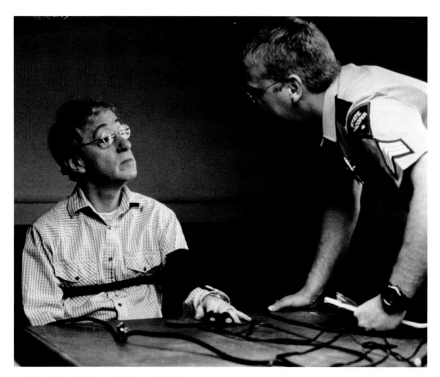

STILL FROM 'PICKING UP THE PIECES' (2000)
Officer Bobo (Kiefer Sutherland) interrogates Tex
Cowley (Woody Allen) to find the whereabouts of his
mistress, who is also Tex's wife. / Polizist Bobo (Kiefer
Sutherland) verhört Tex Cowley (Woody Allen), um
herauszufinden, wo seine Geliebte steckt – die zufällig
auch Cowleys Ehefrau ist. / Le policier Bobo (Kiefer
Sutherland) interroge Tex Cowley (Woody Allen) pour
retrouver la trace de sa maîtresse, qui n'est autre que la
femme de Tex.

STILL FROM 'PICKING UP THE PIECES' (2000)
Tex is a butcher who kills his unfaithful wife and then
learns that her severed hand may have miraculous
properties. / Tex ist ein Metzger, der seine untreue
Frau umbringt und dann herausfindet, dass ihre
abgetrennte Hand möglicherweise wundersame
Fähigkeiten besitzt. / Après avoir tué et découpé en
morceaux son épouse infidèle, Tex le boucher découvre
que la main de la défunte a peut-être des propriétés
miraculeuses.

STILL FROM 'THE CURSE OF THE JADE SCORPION' (2001)
Voltan Polgar (David Ogden Stiers) hypnotizes CW and Betty Ann Fitzgerald (Helen Hunt) so that they fall in love. / Voltan Polgar (David Ogden Stiers) hypnotisiert CW und Betty Ann Fitzgerald (Helen Hunt), sodass sie sich ineinander verlieben. / Hypnotisés par Voltan Polgar (David Ogden Stiers), CW et Betty Ann Fitzgerald (Helen Hunt) tombent amoureux l'un de l'autre.

PAGES 148/149
STILL FROM 'THE CURSE OF THE JADE SCORPION' (2001)
CW Briggs (Woody Allen) is a top insurance investigator in this homage to film noir and screwball comedies of the 1940s. / In dieser Hommage an den *Film noir* und die Screwball-Komödien der 1940er-Jahre spielt Woody Allen den erstklassigen Versicherungsdetektiv CW Briggs. / Dans cet hommage au film noir et aux comédies loufoques des années 1940, Woody Allen incarne CW Briggs, l'enquêteur vedette d'une compagnie d'assurance.

"I, from my personal point of view, feel that maybe—and there are many candidates for this—but [The Curse of the Jade Scorpion] may be the worst film I've made. It kills me to have a cast so gifted and not be able to come through for them. They put their trust in me."
Woody Allen in 2006

STILL FROM 'THE CURSE OF THE JADE SCORPION' (2001)
Charlize Theron plays a femme fatale who tries to seduce CW because she has never been refused by an ugly man before. / Charlize Theron spielt eine Femme fatale, die CW zu verführen versucht, weil sie noch nie zuvor von einem hässlichen Mann abgewiesen wurde. / Vexée d'être éconduite par un homme laid, la femme fatale (Charlize Theron) tente de séduire CW.

„Ich, aus meiner ganz persönlichen Sicht, meine - und dafür gibt es viele Kandidaten -, dass [Im Bann des Jade Skorpions] vielleicht der schlechteste Film ist, den ich je gemacht habe. Es bringt mich um, eine so talentierte Besetzung zu haben und ihnen dann nichts zu bieten. Sie hatten mir ihr Vertrauen geschenkt."
Woody Allen 2006

« Il y a beaucoup de candidats à ce titre, mais personnellement, je pense que [Le Sortilège du scorpion de jade] est peut-être mon plus mauvais film. J'enrage d'avoir eu des acteurs aussi doués et de ne pas avoir été à la hauteur, alors qu'ils me faisaient confiance. »
Woody Allen en 2006

PAGES 152/153
STILL FROM 'HOLLYWOOD ENDING' (2002)
"The biggest personal shock to me of all the movies that
I've done is that 'Hollywood Ending' was not thought of
as a first-rate, extraordinary comedy ... I was stunned
that it met with any resistance at all."—Woody Allen
(2005) / „Für mich persönlich war der größte
Schock bei allen Filmen, die ich gedreht habe, dass
man *Hollywood Ending* nicht als erstklassige,
außergewöhnliche Komödie betrachtete ... Ich war völlig
baff, dass es überhaupt irgendwelchen Widerstand
gab." — Woody Allen (2005) /« Parmi tous les films que
j'ai faits, le plus grand choc pour moi a été que
Hollywood Ending ne soit pas considéré comme une
comédie hors pair. [...] J'ai été abasourdi par la
résistance qu'il a rencontrée, aussi faible fût-elle. »
— Woody Allen (2005)

*"I do all my films for my own personal reasons, and
I hope that people will like them and I'm always
gratified when I hear they do. But if they don't,
there's nothing I can do about that because I don't
set out to make them for approval—I like approval,
but I don't make them for approval."*
Woody Allen in 2006

STILL FROM 'ANYTHING ELSE' (2003)
Young comedy writer Jerry (Jason Biggs) is in love with neurotic, dangerous Amanda (Christina Ricci), who professes love for him but shies away whenever they begin to make love. / Der junge Comedy-Autor Jerry (Jason Biggs) ist in die gefährliche Neurotikerin Amanda (Christina Ricci) verliebt, die ihm zwar ihre Liebe gesteht, sich aber stets von ihm zurückzieht, wenn es um die körperliche Seite der Liebe geht. / Jeune auteur comique, Jerry (Jason Biggs) est amoureux d'Amanda (Christina Ricci), petite amie névrosée qui ne se laisse pas toucher malgré les sentiments qu'elle prétend éprouver.

„Ich mache alle meine Filme aus persönlichen Gründen, und ich hoffe, dass sie den Leuten gefallen, und es freut mich immer, wenn ich höre, dass dem so ist. Aber wenn es nicht der Fall ist, dann kann ich daran nichts ändern, denn ich mache sie ja nicht, um zu gefallen. Ich mag Beifall, aber ich mache sie nicht um des Beifalls willen."
Woody Allen 2006

« Je fais des films pour des raisons personnelles. Évidemment, j'espère qu'ils plairont au public et je suis heureux quand c'est le cas. Mais sinon, je n'y peux rien, car je ne fais pas des films pour être approuvé. J'aime être approuvé, mais ce n'est pas une fin en soi. »
Woody Allen en 2006

STILL FROM 'ANYTHING ELSE' (2003)
Frustrated, Jerry follows Amanda, trying to discover the
truth about her. / Frustriert folgt Jerry Amanda, um die
Wahrheit über sie herauszufinden. / Frustré, Jerry suit
Amanda dans l'espoir de découvrir son secret.

STILL FROM 'ANYTHING ELSE' (2003)
David Dobel (Woody Allen) mentors Jerry and gives
him writing advice: "If you are going to steal, steal from
the best." / David Dobel (Woody Allen) gibt Jerry
persönliche und berufliche Ratschläge: „Wenn du schon
klaust, dann klau von den Besten." / Le mentor de Jerry,
David Dobel (Woody Allen), lui donne le conseil suivant:
« Si tu veux piquer des idées, pique-les aux meilleurs
auteurs. »

STILL FROM 'MELINDA AND MELINDA' (2004)
Is life essentially comic or tragic? In the comic version
of this story, married Hobie (Will Ferrell) is in love with
Melinda (Radha Mitchell). Here they are with Walt
(Steve Carell). / Ist das Leben im Grunde komisch oder
tragisch? In der komischen Version dieser Geschichte
ist der verheiratete Hobie (Will Ferrell) in Melinda
(Radha Mitchell) verliebt. Hier sind beide mit Walt
(Steve Carell) zu sehen. / La vie est-elle essentiellement
comique ou tragique ? Dans la version comique de
l'histoire, un homme marié, Hobie (Will Ferrell), est
amoureux de Melinda (Radha Mitchell), ici assise à
la gauche de Walt (Steve Carell).

*"Where 90 percent of everything fails is in the
writing. It doesn't usually fail in the acting and it
doesn't usually fail in the directing. It fails in the
writing."*
Woody Allen in 1988

*„90 Prozent von allem geht beim Schreiben
schief. Normalerweise geht es nicht beim
Schauspielerischen schief und normalerweise auch
nicht in der Regie. Es geht beim Buch schief."*
Woody Allen 1988

*« Quand c'est raté, c'est dû à 90 pour cent au
scénario. Le problème ne réside généralement
pas dans l'interprétation ni dans la réalisation.
C'est une question d'écriture. »*
Woody Allen en 1988

STILL FROM 'MELINDA AND MELINDA' (2004)
In the tragic version, Melinda is romanced by Ellis
Moonsong (Chiwetel Ejiofor). / In der tragischen
Version wird Melinda von Ellis Moonsong (Chiwetel
Ejiofor) umgarnt. / Dans la version tragique, Melinda
est courtisée par Ellis Moonsong (Chiwetel Ejiofor).

PAGES 160/161
STILL FROM 'MATCH POINT' (2005)
Newlyweds Chris (Jonathan Rhys Meyers) and Chloe
Wilton (Emily Mortimer) in their London apartment
overlooking the Thames. This film is Allen's most
profitable and one of his most critically praised. / Das
frischverheiratete Paar Chris (Jonathan Rhys Meyers)
und Chloe Wilton (Emily Mortimer) in seiner Londoner
Wohnung mit Blick auf die Themse. Dieser Film spielte
von allen Filmen Woody Allens nicht nur die höchsten
Gewinne ein, sondern gehörte auch zu jenen, die von
den Kritikern am höchsten gelobt wurden. / Les jeunes
mariés, Chris (Jonathan Rhys Meyers) et Chloe Wilton
(Emily Mortimer), dans leur appartenant londonien
surplombant la Tamise. Ce film, le plus lucratif de la
carrière de Woody Allen, est également l'un des plus
applaudis.

STILL FROM 'MATCH POINT' (2005)
Chris, a tennis professional, befriends wealthy Tom
Hewett (Matthew Goode) and eventually marries into
the family. / Tennis-Profi Chris freundet sich mit dem
wohlhabenden Tom Hewett (Matthew Goode) an und
heiratet schließlich in dessen Familie ein. / Tennisman
professionnel, Chris se lie d'amitié avec le riche Tom
Hewett (Matthew Goode)... et finit par épouser sa sœur.

"There are two kinds of mystery-murder stories.
There's the kind that's the airplane-read-type
mystery story, and there's the type—I'm not making
any comparison here—where the murder is used
in a more significant way, like in Macbeth or Crime
and Punishment or The Brothers Karamazov;
there's a murder but it's used philosophically and
not as a whodunit. I was trying [in Match Point] to
give a little substance to the story so it wasn't just
a genre piece."
Woody Allen in 2005

„Es gibt zwei Arten von Kriminalgeschichten.
Zum einen sind da die Krimis, die man im Flugzeug
liest, und zum anderen jene Art – ich will hier
keinen Vergleich anstellen –, wo der Mord eine
bedeutendere Rolle spielt, wie in Macbeth oder
Schuld und Sühne oder Die Brüder Karamasow.
Dort gibt es auch einen Mord, aber er wird
philosophisch eingesetzt und nicht nur um des
Rätsels willen, wer der Mörder war. Ich versuchte
[in Match Point], der Geschichte ein wenig
Substanz zu verleihen, damit es nicht nur ein
Genrestück wurde."
Woody Allen 2005

STILL FROM 'MATCH POINT' (2005)
When Chris meets Tom's fiancée, Nola (Scarlett Johansson), he is immediately smitten and they begin a passionate affair. / Als Chris Toms Verlobte Nola (Scarlett Johansson) kennenlernt, ist er sofort völlig hingerissen von ihr und beginnt eine leidenschaftliche Affäre. / Lorsqu'il rencontre Nola (Scarlett Johansson), la fiancée de Tom, Chris a le coup de foudre et entame avec elle une liaison passionnée.

« Il y a deux catégories d'histoires de meurtres. Il y a celles qu'on lit dans l'avion, et il y a celles, sans commune mesure, où le meurtre a une portée plus significative, comme dans Macbeth, Crime et Châtiment ou Les Frères Karamazov. Il y a un meurtre, mais dans un but philosophique, et non pour qu'il y ait un mystère à élucider. [Dans Match Point,] j'ai essayé de donner un peu de substance à l'histoire pour que ce ne soit pas juste un film de genre. »
Woody Allen en 2005

"I feel that I could do dramatic films now with the same confidence that I had when I was rattling off comic films, and I feel people will now accept them. I mean, Match Point made more money than any film I've done in my life."
Woody Allen in 2006

„Ich habe das Gefühl, dass ich heutzutage dramatische Filme mit dem gleichen Selbstvertrauen machen könnte, das ich besaß, als ich lustige Filme herunterleierte, und ich habe das Gefühl, dass die Leute sie heute akzeptieren. Immerhin spielte Match Point mehr Geld ein als jeder andere Film, den ich in meinem Leben gedreht habe."
Woody Allen 2006

« J'ai le sentiment que je pourrais désormais faire des films dramatiques avec la même assurance que quand j'alignais les films comiques, et j'ai l'impression que le public est prêt à les accepter. Après tout, Match Point est celui qui a rapporté le plus d'argent. »
Woody Allen en 2006

STILL FROM 'MATCH POINT' (2005)
Nola's demands threaten to ruin Chris's comfortable moneyed life, so eventually he plans her murder. / Chris sieht sein angenehmes Leben im Wohlstand durch Nolas Ansprüche gefährdet und plant schließlich ihre Ermordung. / Face aux exigences de Nola, qui menace son existence confortable, Chris finit par décider de la tuer.

PAGES 166/167
ON THE SET OF 'MATCH POINT' (2005)
While directing on set, it is not uncommon for Allen to find a neutral space and to just spend some time alone thinking about the film. / Während er Regie führt, kommt es nicht selten vor, dass sich Allen ein stilles Eckchen sucht, um für sich allein über den Film nachzudenken. / Pendant le tournage, il n'est pas rare que Woody Allen cherche un endroit tranquille pour réfléchir au film.

STILL FROM 'SCOOP' (2006)
In this comedy-mystery, student journalist Sondra
(Scarlett Johansson) is told by a ghost that Peter Lyman
(Hugh Jackman) is a serial killer, but she falls for him. /
In diesem Kriminallustspiel erfährt die angehende
Journalistin Sondra (Scarlett Johansson) von einem
Geist, dass Peter Lyman (Hugh Jackman) ein
Serienmörder ist, verliebt sich aber dennoch in ihn. /
Entre polar et comédie : avertie par un revenant que
Peter Lyman (Hugh Jackman) est un tueur en série,
Sondra (Scarlett Johansson), une journaliste en herbe,
mène l'enquête et succombe à son charme.

*"I've been given more opportunities than anybody.
I've been given the money and the freedom for 35
years now to make whatever I wanted: A musical?
OK. A detective story? Fine. A drama? Absolutely.
Another drama, even though the first one failed?
Go ahead. Whatever you want. So there's been no
reason for me not to make great films … I've had
carte blanche for 35 years and I've never made a
great film. It's just not in me to make a great film;
I don't have the depth of vision to do it."*
Woody Allen in 2005

*„Ich habe mehr Chancen bekommen als irgendein
anderer Mensch. Man hat mir 35 Jahre lang Geld
gegeben und die Freiheit, alles zu machen, was ich
wollte: ein Musical? Okay. Ein Krimi? In Ordnung.
Ein Drama? Kein Problem. Noch ein Drama, obwohl
das erste komplett durchfiel? Mach nur. Was immer
du willst. Es gibt also keinen Grund, warum ich*

STILL FROM 'SCOOP' (2006)
Magician Sid Waterman (Woody Allen) pretends to be Sondra's father so that they can investigate Peter Lyman together. / Der Zauberkünstler Sid Waterman (Woody Allen) gibt sich als Sondras Vater aus, damit sie beide gemeinsam Nachforschungen über Peter Lyman anstellen können. / Le magicien Sid Waterman (Woody Allen) prétend être le père de Sondra pour pouvoir enquêter avec elle.

keine überragenden Filme hätte machen sollen ... Ich hatte 35 Jahre lang einen Freibrief, und ich hab nie einen großen Film gemacht. Es steckt einfach nicht in mir, einen großen Film zu machen. Mir fehlt schlicht die visionäre Tiefe.“
Woody Allen 2005

« J'ai eu énormément de chance. Pendant 35 ans, on m'a donné les moyens et la liberté de faire tout ce que je voulais. Une comédie musicale ? D'accord. Un polar ? Pas de problème. Un drame ? Mais bien sûr. Un autre drame, alors que le premier a fait un four ? Allez-y, faites ce que vous voulez. Alors il n'y a pas eu de raison pour que je ne fasse pas de grands films. [...] J'ai eu carte blanche pendant 35 ans et je n'ai jamais fait de grand film. C'est juste que je n'ai pas cela en moi. Je n'ai pas la profondeur nécessaire. »
Woody Allen en 2005

STILL FROM 'CASSANDRA'S DREAM' (2007)
Ian (Ewan McGregor) and Terry (Colin Farrell) are South
London brothers in need of money—one for a business
proposition, the other to clear gambling debts. / Ian
(Ewan McGregor) und Terry (Colin Farrell) sind zwei
Brüder in Südlondon, die dringend Geld brauchen: der
eine für ein Geschäftsvorhaben, der andere, um
Spielschulden zu bezahlen. / Ian (Ewan McGregor) et
Terry (Colin Farrell), deux frères des faubourgs
londoniens ayant cruellement besoin d'argent, l'un
pour faire des affaires, l'autre pour éponger ses
dettes de jeu.

STILL FROM 'CASSANDRA'S DREAM' (2007)
Their successful uncle Howard (Tom Wilkinson) offers
them a murderous quid pro quo. / Ihr erfolgreicher
Onkel Howard (Tom Wilkinson) bietet ihnen ein
mörderisches Tauschgeschäft an. / Howard
(Tom Wilkinson), l'oncle qui a fait fortune, leur propose
un macabre marché.

PAGES 172/173
STILL FROM 'CASSANDRA'S DREAM' (2007)
The brothers reluctantly decide to carry out the killing,
but it will irrevocably change their relationship. /
Widerwillig entschließen sich die Brüder, den Mord zu
begehen, aber die Tat wird ihre Beziehung zueinander
unwiderruflich verändern. / Acceptant à contrecœur de
commettre un meurtre, les deux frères verront leur
relation s'altérer à jamais.

**STILL FROM 'VICKY CRISTINA BARCELONA'
(2008)**
The artist Juan Antonio (Javier Bardem) approaches the
free-spirited, vacationing Cristina (Scarlett Johansson). /
Der Künstler Juan Antonio (Javier Bardem) macht sich
an die unkonventionelle Urlauberin Cristina (Scarlett
Johansson) heran. / L'artiste Juan Antonio (Javier
Bardem) fait des avances à Cristina (Scarlett
Johansson), touriste américaine peu farouche.

*"You hire Ian Holm and Gena Rowlands, what does
it take to get superb performances out of them?
Nothing. You just have to tell them what time to
show up and provide the coffee and doughnuts.
And that's what I've been doing my whole life,
hiring people who can do it."*
Woody Allen in 2005

*„Man engagiert Ian Holm und Gena Rowlands,
und was muss man tun, um ihnen eine großartige
schauspielerische Leistung zu entlocken? Nichts.
Man sagt ihnen, wann sie erscheinen müssen, und
stellt den Kaffee und die Donuts bereit. Das hab
ich mein ganzes Leben lang gemacht: Leute
engagieren, die es können."*
Woody Allen 2005

**STILL FROM 'VICKY CRISTINA BARCELONA'
(2008)**
Juan also approaches Cristina's more straightlaced
travel companion, Vicky (Rebecca Hall). / Juan macht
sich auch an Cristinas ein wenig zugeknöpftere
Mitreisende Vicky (Rebecca Hall) heran. / Juan tente
également de séduire Vicky (Rebecca Hall), sa
compagne de voyage plus collet monté.

*« Quand vous travaillez avec Ian Holm et Gena
Rowlands, que faut-il faire pour obtenir d'eux une
prestation impeccable ? Rien. Il suffit de leur dire à
quelle heure ils commencent et de prévoir du café
et des croissants. C'est ce que j'ai fait toute ma vie,
travailler avec des gens qui savent faire leur
métier. »*
Woody Allen en 2005

**STILL FROM 'VICKY CRISTINA BARCELONA'
(2008)**
Complications arise when Juan's emotionally troubled
ex-wife (Penélope Cruz) appears. / Als Juans emotional
gestörte Exfrau (Penélope Cruz) auftaucht, wird es
kompliziert. / La situation se complique lorsque surgit
l'ex-femme de Juan (Penélope Cruz), créature pour le
moins perturbée.

*"If tomorrow I couldn't get financing I would be
very happy to write plays, very happy to sit home
and try to write a novel and maybe under those
circumstances try to write an autobiography or a
memoir. I just like to work, to write."*
Woody Allen in 2006

*„Wenn man mir morgen den Geldhahn zudrehen
würde, dann wäre ich sehr glücklich damit,
Theaterstücke zu schreiben, zu Hause zu sitzen
und einen Roman zu schreiben oder unter diesen
Umständen vielleicht eine Autobiografie oder
Memoiren zu schreiben. Mir macht es einfach Spaß
zu arbeiten, zu schreiben."*
Woody Allen 2006

ON THE SET OF 'VICKY CRISTINA BARCELONA' (2008)
The film is the fourth Allen film in a row to be set outside the United States and the first shot in Spain. / Der Film ist der vierte Allen-Film in Folge, der außerhalb der USA spielt, und der erste, der in Spanien gedreht wurde. / C'est le quatrième film d'affilée tourné hors des États-Unis et le premier réalisé en Espagne.

« Si demain, je n'obtenais plus de financement, je serais très heureux de rester chez moi pour essayer d'écrire des pièces, un roman ou même une autobiographie ou des mémoires. J'aime tout simplement travailler et écrire. »
Woody Allen en 2006

PAGE 178
STILL FROM 'ZELIG' (1983)
Zelig (Woody Allen) with Eugene O'Neill. / Zelig (Woody Allen) mit Eugene O'Neill. / Zelig (Woody Allen) avec le dramaturge Eugene O'Neill.

3

CHRONOLOGY

CHRONOLOGIE

CHRONOLOGIE

CHRONOLOGY

1 December 1935 Born Allan Stewart Konigsberg in New York.

1952 Changes name when he begins to place quips in New York newspaper columns. Hired by publicist David Alber to write one-liners for celebrity clients.

1953 Begins writing for television (Pat Boone, Buddy Hackett, Garry Moore, Sid Caesar) with collaborators like Danny Simon, Neil Simon, Larry Gelbart, and Mel Brooks.

15 March 1956 Marries Harlene Rosen (divorced 1962). Briefly writes in Hollywood for NBC.

1960 Becomes client of managers Jack Rollins and Charles Joffe, who initiate his career as a stand-up comedian.

1965 Writes and appears in *What's New Pussycat?*, directed by Clive Donner.

1966 2 February: Marries Louise Lasser (divorced 1969). Dubs comic dialogue on Japanese film *Kagi No Kagi*, re-titling it *What's Up, Tiger Lily?* 17 November: *Don't Drink the Water* opens on Broadway; it runs for 598 performances.

1967 Appears in *Casino Royale*.

12 February 1968 *Play It Again, Sam* opens on Broadway; it runs for 453 performances.

1969 Writes, directs, and stars in *Take the Money and Run*.

1971 *Getting Even*, a collection of prose pieces mostly from *The New Yorker*, published.

1975 *Without Feathers*, a collection of prose writings, published.

1977 Writes, directs, and stars in *Annie Hall* (wins Oscars for best screenplay, direction).

1980 *Side Effects*, a collection of prose writings, published. Begins relationship with Mia Farrow (ended 1992).

27 April 1981 *The Floating Light Bulb* opens at Lincoln Center; it runs for 65 performances.

1986 Writes, directs, and stars in *Hannah and Her Sisters* (wins Oscar for best screenplay).

1987 Appears in *King Lear*, directed by Jean-Luc Godard.

1993 Loses custody of three children to Mia Farrow following her publicized accusation of child abuse. Writes, directs, and stars in *Manhattan Murder Mystery*.

6 March 1995 *Central Park West*, a one-act play and part of *Death Defying Acts*, opens at the Variety Arts Theater; it runs for 343 performances.

22 December 1997 Marries Soon-Yi Previn. They later adopt two daughters.

15 May 2003 *Writer's Block* opens off-Broadway for a limited run.

22 November 2004 *A Second Hand Memory* opens off-Broadway for a limited run.

2005 Writes and directs *Match Point*.

2007 *Mere Anarchy* and *The Insanity Defense*, prose collections, published.

2008 Writes and directs *Vicky Cristina Barcelona*.

ON THE SET OF 'THE CURSE OF THE JADE SCORPION' (2001)

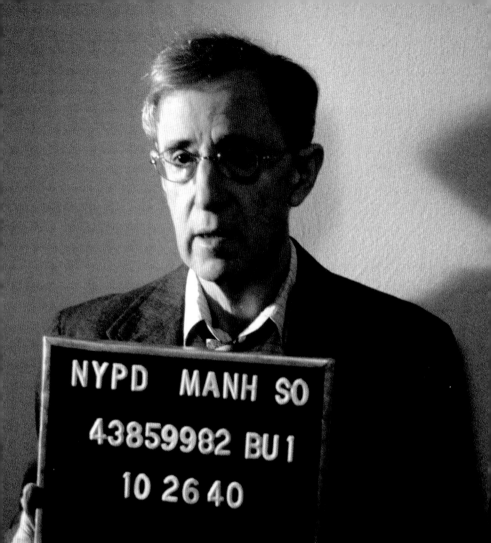

CHRONOLOGIE

1. Dezember 1935 Er wird als Allan Stewart Konigsberg in New York geboren.

1952 Ändert seinen Namen, als er beginnt, Witze für New Yorker Zeitungskolumnen zu schreiben. Wird von dem Publizisten David Alber engagiert, um über seine prominenten Klienten zu schreiben.

1953 Beginnt, zusammen mit Danny Simon, Neil Simon, Larry Gelbart und Mel Brooks, für das Fernsehen zu schreiben (Pat Boone, Buddy Hackett, Garry Moore, Sid Caesar).

15. März 1956 Heiratet Harlene Rosen (Scheidung 1962). Schreibt in Hollywood kurze Zeit für NBC.

1960 Wird Klient der Manager Jack Rollins und Charles Joffe, die seine Karriere als Stand-up-Comedian in Gang bringen.

1965 Schreibt das Drehbuch zu *Was gibt's Neues, Pussy?* und spielt in dem Film unter der Regie von Clive Donner mit.

1966 2. Februar: Heiratet Louise Lasser (Scheidung 1969). Synchronisiert witzige neue Dialoge zu dem japanischen Film *Kokusai himitsu keisatsu: Kagi no Kagi*, dem er den neuen Titel *What's Up, Tiger Lily?* gibt. 17. November: *Vorsicht, Trinkwasser!* feiert Premiere am Broadway und läuft 598 Vorstellungen lang.

1967 Tritt in dem Film *Casino Royale* auf.

12. Februar 1968 *Mach's noch einmal, Sam* feiert Premiere am Broadway und läuft 453 Vorstellungen lang.

1969 Schreibt das Drehbuch für *Woody, der Unglücksrabe*, führt Regie und spielt die Hauptrolle.

1971 *Wie du dir, so ich mir*, eine Sammlung kurzer Prosastücke hauptsächlich aus dem *New Yorker*, erscheint.

STILL FROM 'THE CURSE OF THE JADE SCORPION' (2001)

1975 *Ohne Leit kein Freud*, eine weitere Sammlung von Prosatexten, erscheint.

1977 Schreibt das Drehbuch für *Der Stadtneurotiker*, führt Regie und spielt eine der Hauptrollen. Der Film erhält den „Oscar" für das beste Drehbuch und die beste Regie.

1980 *Nebenwirkungen*, eine weitere Sammlung von Prosatexten, erscheint. Beginnt eine Beziehung mit Mia Farrow (die 1992 endet).

27. April 1981 *The Floating Light Bulb* feiert Premiere im Lincoln Center und läuft 65 Vorstellungen lang.

1986 Schreibt das Drehbuch für *Hannah und ihre Schwestern*, führt Regie und spielt eine der Hauptrollen. Der Film erhält den „Oscar" für das beste Drehbuch.

1987 Tritt in *King Lear* unter der Regie von Jean-Luc Godard auf.

1993 Verliert das Sorgerecht für drei gemeinsame Kinder an Mia Farrow, nachdem sie ihn öffentlich des Kindesmissbrauchs bezichtigte. Er schreibt das Drehbuch für *Manhattan Murder Mystery*, führt Regie und spielt eine der Hauptrollen.

6. März 1995 *Central Park West*, ein Einakter und Teil von *Death Defying Acts*, feiert Premiere im Variety Arts Theater und läuft 343 Vorstellungen lang.

22. Dezember 1997 Heiratet Soon-Yi Previn. Das Paar adoptiert später zwei Töchter.

15. Mai 2003 *Writer's Block* wird für begrenzte Zeit „off Broadway" aufgeführt.

22. November 2004 *A Second Hand Memory* wird für begrenzte Zeit „off Broadway" aufgeführt.

2005 Schreibt das Drehbuch zu *Match Point* und führt Regie.

2007 Die Prosasammlungen *Pure Anarchie* und *The Insanity Defense* erscheinen.

2008 Schreibt das Drehbuch zu *Vicky Cristina Barcelona* und führt Regie.

CHRONOLOGIE

1er décembre 1935 Naît à New York sous le nom d'Allan Stewart Konigsberg.

1952 Commence à inventer des mots d'esprits sous le pseudonyme de Woody Allen, d'abord pour des chroniqueurs de journaux new-yorkais, puis pour des célébrités par le biais de l'agent David Alber.

1953 Se met à écrire pour la télévision (Pat Boone, Buddy Hackett, Garry Moore, Sid Caesar) avec des collaborateurs tels que Danny et Neil Simon, Larry Gelbart et Mel Brooks.

15 mars 1956 Épouse Harlene Rosen (divorce en 1962). Écrit quelque temps pour NBC à Hollywood.

1960 Débute une carrière dans le stand-up grâce à ses agents Jack Rollins et Charles Joffe.

1965 Écrit et joue dans *Quoi de neuf, Pussycat ?*, réalisé par Clive Donner.

1966 2 février : épouse Louise Lasser (divorce en 1969). Réécrit des dialogues comiques pour le film japonais *Kagi No Kagi*, rebaptisé *Lily la tigresse*. 17 novembre : première de *Don't Drink the Water* à Broadway (598 représentations).

1967 Joue dans le film *Casino Royale*.

12 février 1968 Première d'*Une aspirine pour deux* (*Play It Again, Sam*) à Broadway (453 représentations).

1969 Écrit, réalise et interprète *Prends l'oseille et tire-toi*.

1971 Publication de *Pour en finir une bonne fois pour toutes avec la culture* (*Getting Even*), recueil de textes en prose principalement parus dans *The New Yorker*.

1975 Publication de *Dieu, Shakespeare et moi* (*Without Feathers*), recueil de textes en prose.

1977 Écrit, réalise et joue dans *Annie Hall* (oscars du Meilleur scénario et du Meilleur réalisateur).

1980 Publication de *Destins tordus* (*Side Effects*), recueil de textes en prose. Rencontre avec Mia Farrow (sa compagne jusqu'en 1992).

27 avril 1981 Première de *L'Ampoule magique* (*The Floating Light Bulb*) au Lincoln Center (65 représentations).

1986 Écrit, réalise et joue dans *Hannah et ses sœurs* (oscar du Meilleur scénario).

1987 Joue dans *King Lear* de Jean-Luc Godard.

1993 Perd la garde de ses trois enfants suite à l'accusation de pédophilie très médiatisée proférée par Mia Farrow. Écrit, réalise et joue dans *Meurtre mystérieux à Manhattan*.

6 mars 1995 Première de *Central Park West*, pièce en un acte faisant partie du spectacle *Adultères* (*Death Defying Acts*), au Variety Arts Theater (343 représentations).

22 décembre 1997 Épouse Soon-Yi Previn, avec laquelle il adoptera deux filles.

15 mai 2003 Première de *Writer's Block* pour quelques représentations.

22 novembre 2004 Première de *Puzzle* (*A Second-Hand Memory*) pour quelques représentations.

2005 Écrit et réalise *Match Point*.

2007 Publication de *L'erreur est humaine* (*Mere Anarchy*) et de *The Insanity Defense*, recueils de textes en prose.

2008 Écrit et réalise *Vicky Cristina Barcelona*.

ON THE SET OF 'EVERYTHING YOU ALWAYS WANTED TO KNOW ABOUT SEX* (*BUT WERE AFRAID TO ASK)' (1972)

WOODY ALLEN
DIANE KEATON
MICHAEL MURPHY
MARIEL HEMINGWAY
MERYL STREEP
ANNE BYRNE

MANHATTAN

"MANHATTAN" Musik GEORGE GERSHWIN
Eine JACK ROLLINS-CHARLES H. JOFFE Produktion
Drehbuch WOODY ALLEN und MARSHALL BRICKMAN Regie WOODY ALLEN
Produktion CHARLES H. JOFFE Produktionsleitung ROBERT GREENHUT Kamera GORDON WILLIS

United Artists
a Transamerica Company   Copyright © 1979 United Artists Corporation

4

FILMOGRAPHY

FILMOGRAFIE

FILMOGRAPHIE

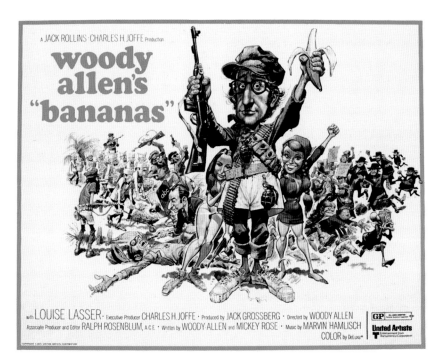

What's New Pussycat? (dt. *Was gibt's Neues, Pussy?,* **fr.** *Quoi de neuf, Pussycat ?,* **1965)**
Victor Shakapopolis. Writer/Drehbuch/scénario: Woody Allen. Director/Regie/réalisation: Clive Donner.

What's Up, Tiger Lily? (fr. *Lily la tigresse,* **1966)**
Writer and dubbing director/Drehbuch und Synchronregie/scénario et doublage: Woody Allen.

Casino Royale (1967)
Jimmy Bond/Dr. Noah. Directors/Regie/réalisation: John Huston, Ken Hughes, Val Guest, Robert Parrish, Joseph McGrath.

Take the Money and Run (dt. *Woody, der Unglücksrabe,* **fr.** *Prends l'oseille et tire-toi,* **1969)**
Virgil Starkwell. Writers/Drehbuch/scénario: Woody Allen, Mickey Rose. Director/Regie/réalisation: Woody Allen.

Bananas (1971)
Fielding Mellish. Writers/Drehbuch/scénario: Woody Allen, Mickey Rose. Director/Regie/réalisation: Woody Allen.

Play It Again, Sam (dt. *Mach's noch einmal, Sam,* **fr.** *Tombe les filles et tais-toi,* **1972)**
Allan Felix. Writer/Drehbuch/scénario: Woody Allen. Director/Regie/réalisation: Herbert Ross.

Everything You Always Wanted to Know About Sex* (*But Were Afraid to Ask) (dt. *Was Sie schon immer über Sex wissen wollten* [*aber bisher nicht zu fragen wagten],* **fr.** *Tout ce que vous avez toujours voulu savoir sur le sexe sans jamais oser le demander,* **1972)**
Fool/Narr/le bouffon; Fabrizio; Victor; The Timid Sperm/Spermium/le spermatozoïde. Writer and director/Drehbuch und Regie/scénario et réalisation: Woody Allen.

Sleeper (dt. *Der Schläfer,* **fr.** *Woody et les robots,* **1973)**
Miles Monroe. Writers/Drehbuch/scénario: Woody Allen, Marshall Brickman. Director/Regie/réalisation: Woody Allen.

Love and Death (dt. *Die letzte Nacht des Boris Gruschenko,* **fr.** *Guerre et Amour,* **1975)**
Boris. Writer and director/Drehbuch und Regie/scénario et réalisation: Woody Allen.

The Front (dt. *Der Strohmann*, fr. *Le Prête-nom*, 1976)
Howard Prince. Director/Regie/réalisation: Martin Ritt.

Annie Hall (dt. *Der Stadtneurotiker*, 1977)
Alvy Singer. Writers/Drehbuch/scénario: Woody Allen, Marshall Brickman. Director/Regie/réalisation: Woody Allen.

Interiors (dt. *Innenleben*, fr. *Intérieurs*, 1978)
Writer and director/Drehbuch und Regie/scénario et réalisation: Woody Allen.

Manhattan (1979)
Isaac Davis. Writers/Drehbuch/scénario: Woody Allen, Marshall Brickman. Director/Regie/réalisation: Woody Allen.

Stardust Memories (1980)
Sandy Bates. Writer and director/Drehbuch und Regie/scénario et réalisation: Woody Allen.

A Midsummer Night's Sex Comedy (dt. *Eine Sommernachts-Sexkomödie*, fr. *Comédie érotique d'une nuit d'été*, 1982)

Andrew Hobbes. Writer and director/Drehbuch und Regie/scénario et réalisation: Woody Allen.

Zelig (1983)
Leonard Zelig. Writer and director/Drehbuch und Regie/scénario et réalisation: Woody Allen.

Broadway Danny Rose (1984)
Danny Rose. Writer and director/Drehbuch und Regie/scénario et réalisation: Woody Allen.

The Purple Rose of Cairo (fr. *La Rose pourpre du Caire*, 1985)
Writer and director/Drehbuch und Regie/scénario et réalisation: Woody Allen.

Hannah and Her Sisters (dt. *Hannah und ihre Schwestern*, fr. *Hannah et ses sœurs*, 1986)
Mickey. Writer and director/Drehbuch und Regie/scénario et réalisation: Woody Allen.

Radio Days (1987)
Narrator/Erzähler/narrateur. Writer and director/Drehbuch und Regie/scénario et réalisation: Woody Allen.

"ANNIE HALL" AA
A nervous romance.

WOODY ALLEN
DIANE KEATON
TONY ROBERTS
CAROL KANE
PAUL SIMON
SHELLEY DUVALL
JANET MARGOLIN
CHRISTOPHER WALKEN
COLLEEN DEWHURST

THE YEAR'S MOST HONOURED AND FUNNIEST FILM!

WOODY ALLEN'S 'ANNIE HALL'
ACADEMY AWARDS
BEST FILM
BEST ACTRESS
BEST DIRECTION
BEST SCREENPLAY

'ANNIE HALL'
BRITISH ACADEMY OF FILM AND TELEVISION ARTS AWARDS
BEST FILM · BEST ACTRESS
BEST DIRECTION
BEST SCREENPLAY
BEST FILM EDITING

'ANNIE HALL'

A JACK ROLLINS-CHARLES H. JOFFE PRODUCTION
Written by WOODY ALLEN and MARSHALL BRICKMAN
Directed by WOODY ALLEN
Produced by CHARLES H. JOFFE
United Artists
A Transamerica Company

King Lear (1987)
Mr. Alien. Writer and director/Drehbuch und
Regie/scénario et réalisation: Jean-Luc Godard.

September (1987)
Writer and director/Drehbuch und Regie/scénario
et réalisation: Woody Allen.

**Another Woman (dt. *Eine andere Frau*, fr. *Une
autre femme*, 1988)**
Writer and director/Drehbuch und Regie/scénario
et réalisation: Woody Allen.

**Oedipus Wrecks (dt. *Ödipus ratlos*, fr. *Le
Complot d'Œdipe*) (from *New York Stories* [dt.
aus *New Yorker Geschichten*, fr. court métrage
tiré de *New York Stories*], 1989)**
Sheldon Mills. Writer and director/Drehbuch und
Regie/scénario et réalisation: Woody Allen.

**Crimes and Misdemeanors (dt. *Verbrechen
und andere Kleinigkeiten*, fr. *Crimes et délits*,
1989)**
Cliff Stern. Writer and director/Drehbuch und
Regie/scénario et réalisation: Woody Allen.

Alice (1990)
Writer and director/Drehbuch und Regie/scénario
et réalisation: Woody Allen.

**Scenes from a Mall (dt. *Ein ganz normaler
Hochzeitstag*, fr. *Scènes de ménage dans un
centre commercial*, 1991)**
Nick Fifer. Director/Regie/réalisation: Paul
Mazursky.

**Shadows and Fog (dt. *Schatten und Nebel*,
fr. *Ombres et brouillard*, 1992)**
Kleinman. Writer and director/Drehbuch und
Regie/scénario et réalisation: Woody Allen.

**Husbands and Wives (dt. *Ehemänner und
Ehefrauen*, fr. *Maris et femmes*, 1992)**
Gabe Roth. Writer and director/Drehbuch und
Regie/scénario et réalisation: Woody Allen.

**Manhattan Murder Mystery (fr. *Meurtre
mystérieux à Manhattan*, 1993)**
Larry Lipton. Writers/Drehbuch/scénario: Woody
Allen, Marshall Brickman. Director/Regie/
réalisation: Woody Allen.

**Bullets over Broadway (fr. *Coups de feu sur
Broadway*, 1994)**
Writers/Drehbuch/scénario: Woody Allen,
Douglas McGrath. Director/Regie/réalisation:
Woody Allen.

**Mighty Aphrodite (dt. *Geliebte Aphrodite*,
fr. *Maudite Aphrodite*, 1995)**
Lenny. Writer and director/Drehbuch und Regie/
scénario et réalisation: Woody Allen.

**Everyone Says I Love You (dt. *Alle sagen: I Love
You*, fr. *Tout le monde dit "I love you"*, 1996)**
Joe. Writer and director/Drehbuch und Regie/
scénario et réalisation: Woody Allen.

Deconstructing Harry (dt. *Harry außer sich*, fr. *Harry dans tous ses états*, 1997)
Harry Block. Writer and director/Drehbuch und Regie/scénario et réalisation: Woody Allen.

Wild Man Blues (1998)
Woody Allen. Director/Regie/réalisation: Barbara Kopple.

AntZ (fr. *FourmiZ*, 1998)
Z (Voice/Stimme/voix). Directors/Regie/réalisation: Eric Darnell, Tim Johnson.

The Impostors (dt. *The Impostors – Zwei Hochstapler in Not*, fr. *Les Imposteurs*, 1998)
Theater director/Theaterregisseur/metteur en scène de théâtre. Writer and director/Drehbuch und Regie/scénario et réalisation: Stanley Tucci.

Celebrity (dt. *Celebrity – Schön. Reich. Berühmt*, 1998)
Writer and director/Drehbuch und Regie/scénario et réalisation: Woody Allen.

Sweet and Lowdown (fr. *Accords et désaccords*, 1999)
Writer and director/Drehbuch und Regie/scénario et réalisation: Woody Allen.

Picking Up the Pieces (dt. *Ich hab doch nur meine Frau zerlegt!*, fr. *Morceaux choisis*, 2000)
Tex Cowley. Director/Regie/réalisation: Alfonso Arau.

Small Time Crooks (dt. *Schmalspurganoven*, fr. *Escrocs mais pas trop*, 2000)
Ray. Writer and director/Drehbuch und Regie/scénario et réalisation: Woody Allen.

The Curse of the Jade Scorpion (dt. *Im Bann des Jade Skorpions*, fr. *Le Sortilège du scorpion de jade*, 2001)
CW Briggs. Writer and director/Drehbuch und Regie/scénario et réalisation: Woody Allen.

Hollywood Ending (2002)
Val. Writer and director/Drehbuch und Regie/scénario et réalisation: Woody Allen.

Anything Else (fr. *La Vie et tout le reste*, 2003)
David Dobel. Writer and director/Drehbuch und Regie/scénario et réalisation: Woody Allen.

Melinda and Melinda (dt. *Melinda und Melinda*, fr. *Melinda et Melinda*, 2004)

Writer and director/Drehbuch und Regie/scénario et réalisation: Woody Allen.

Match Point (2005)
Writer and director/Drehbuch und Regie/scénario et réalisation: Woody Allen.

Scoop (dt. *Scoop – Der Knüller*, 2006)
Sid Waterman. Writer and director/Drehbuch und Regie/scénario et réalisation: Woody Allen.

Cassandra's Dream (dt. *Cassandras Traum*, fr. *Le Rêve de Cassandre*, 2007)
Writer and director/Drehbuch und Regie/scénario et réalisation: Woody Allen.

Vicky Cristina Barcelona (2008)
Writer and director/Drehbuch und Regie/scénario et réalisation: Woody Allen.

BIBLIOGRAPHY

Allen, Woody: *The Floating Light Bulb.* New York, 1982.

Allen, Woody (with Marshall Brickman): *Four Films of Woody Allen: Annie Hall, Interiors, Manhattan, Stardust Memories.* New York, 1982.

Allen, Woody: *Getting Even.* New York, 1971.

Allen, Woody: *The Insanity Defense: The Complete Prose.* New York, 2007.

Allen, Woody: *Mere Anarchy.* New York, 2007.

Allen, Woody: *Side Effects.* New York, 1980.

Allen, Woody: *Three Films of Woody Allen: Zelig, Broadway Danny Rose, The Purple Rose of Cairo.* London, 1987.

Allen, Woody: *Three One-Act Plays: Riverside Drive, Old Saybrook, Central Park West.* New York, 2003.

Allen, Woody: *Without Feathers.* New York, 1975.

Baxter, John: *Woody Allen: A Biography.* New York, 2000.

Benayoun, Robert: *The Films of Woody Allen.* Trans. Alexander Walker. New York, 1987.

Bendazzi, Giannalberto: *Woody Allen.* Paris, 1985.

Björkman, Stig: *Woody Allen on Woody Allen: In Conversation with Stig Björkman.* New York, 1993.

Duncan, Paul (as Martin Fitzgerald): *The Pocket Essential Woody Allen.* Harpenden, 2000.

Dureau, Christian: *Woody Allen.* Paris, coll. « Cinépoche », 1986.

Frodon, Jean-Michel: *Woody Allen im Gespräch mit Jean-Michel Frodon.* Zürich, 2005.

Girgus, Sam B.: *The Films of Woody Allen.* Cambridge, 2002.

Guerand, Jean-Philippe: *Woody Allen.* Paris, coll. « Rivages-cinéma », 1995.

Jacobs, Diane: *... But We Need the Eggs: The Magic of Woody Allen.* New York, 1982.

Kapsis, Robert & Coblentz, Kathie (Eds.): *Interviews: Woody Allen.* Oxford, 2006.

Lax, Eric: *Conversations with Woody Allen: His Films, the Movies, and Moviemaking.* New York, 2007.

Lax, Eric: *On Being Funny: Woody Allen and Comedy.* New York, 1975.

Lax, Eric: *Woody Allen: A Biography.* New York, 1991.

Meade, Marion: *The Unruly Life of Woody Allen.* New York, 2000.

Reimertz, Stephan: *Woody Allen. Eine Biographie.* Reinbek, 2000.

Rolandeau, Yannick: *Le Cinéma de Woody Allen.* Lyon, 2006.

Schickel, Richard: *Woody Allen: A Life in Film.* Chicago, 2003.

Schulz, Berndt: *Woody Allen Lexikon. Alles über den Autor, Regisseur, Darsteller, Komiker, Entertainer und Privatmann aus Manhattan.* Berlin, 2000.

Silet, Charles L. P. (Ed.): *The Films of Woody Allen: Critical Essays.* Maryland, 2006.

Skoble, Aeon J. & Conard, Mark T.: *Woody Allen and Philosophy: You Mean My Whole Fallacy Is Wrong?* Chicago, 2004.

Yacowar, Maurice: *Loser Take All: The Comic Art of Woody Allen.* New York, 1979.

IMPRINT

© 2009 TASCHEN GmbH
Hohenzollernring 53, D-50 672 Köln
www.taschen.com

Editor/Picture Research/Layout: Paul Duncan/Wordsmith Solutions
Editorial Coordination: Martin Holz, Cologne
Production Coordination: Nadia Najm, Cologne
German translation: Thomas J. Kinne, Nauheim
French translation: Anne Le Bot, Paris
Multilingual production: www.arnaudbriand.com, Paris
Typeface Design: Sense/Net, Andy Disl and Birgit Eichwede, Cologne

Printed in China
ISBN: 978-3-8365-0851-3

To stay informed about upcoming TASCHEN titles, please request our magazine at www.taschen.com/magazine or write to TASCHEN, Hohenzollernring 53, D-50672 Cologne, Germany; contact@taschen.com; Fax: +49-221-254919. We will be happy to send you a free copy of our magazine, which is filled with information about all of our books.

Copyright